Celebra
Times of
Change

Celebrating
Times of
Change

**A Wiccan Book of Shadows
for Family and Coven Growth**

Stanley J. A. Modrzyk

SAMUEL WEISER, INC.

York Beach, Maine

First published in 1995 by
Samuel Weiser, Inc.
P. O. Box 612
York Beach, ME 03910-0612

Library of Congress Cataloging-in-Publication Data

Modrzyk, Stanley J. A.
    Celebrating times of change / Stanley J.A. Modrzyk.
        p.   cm.
    Sequel to: Turning of the wheel.
    Includes index.
        1. Witchcraft   2. Paganism—Rituals. 3. Rites and cere-
monies.
    I. Title.
BF1566.M6545   1995
299—dc20   95-3719
                                                 CIP

ISBN 0-87728-820-8
BJ

Cover art copyright © 1995 Dorothy Sholeen. Used by kind
permission.

Typeset in 11 point Palatino

Printed in the United States of America

00 99 98 97 96 95
10 9 8 7 6 5 4 3 2 1

The paper used in this publication meets the minimum require-
ments of the American National Standard for Permanence of
Paper for Printed Library Materials Z39.48-1984.

This book is dedicated to Pagan families and their children everywhere—and particularly to my daughter, Elizabeth, who has taught me much. It is through sharing with the children and fostering their awareness that the Craft and all its life-loving beliefs will grow and aid humanity's awakening!

Table of Contents

Foreword

This sequel to the *Turning of the Wheel* (York Beach, ME: Samuel Weiser, Inc., 1993) reveals one coven's way of working and celebrating the rites of passage in all of our lives. For most aspirants, the only way to even see a "book of shadows" is to join and train with a coven. The First Temple of the Craft of W.I.C.A., which has over twenty years of practice of our religion, does not ask this, nor do they claim to have the only way. If you are interested in what exactly witches do and how they do it, then you will benefit from *Celebrating Times of Change: A Wiccan Book of Shadows for Family & Coven Growth*. In a non-dogmatic way, Stan Modrzyk explains his tradition's beliefs, structure, practices, and even covers initiation. So many popular books these days neglect the concept of theurgy, of doing a working from beginning to end and incorporating all the elements necessary for the successful working and practice of the Craft. This book painstakingly reveals all the elements necessary for success, while advocating and encouraging your own interpretation and additions to the basic elements of witchcraft.

For the beginner, this work offers valuable insights into the nature, practice, and structure of the religion of the Craft. For any practitioner secure in their own tradition, a true study of this work can only be of benefit as is any study of comparative religion.

We are once again in a period of blended troth, when the old ways of our pre-Christian ancestors are being researched, reinterpreted, and practiced once again. Books such as this one add to the growing body of lore and knowledge of the old ways in an attempt to bridge the gap between the worlds and reclaim our lost knowledge and heritage.

Live true!
Prudence O. Priest
High Priestess, Amaranth Energies
Elder, Covenant of the Goddess
Elder and Steerswoman of the Ring of Troth
Full Moon, August, 1994

Preface

Starting in 1970, the First Temple of the Craft of W.I.C.A. began as a small coven practicing the Olde Religion— Witchcraft. Originally an offshoot of the Pagan Way tradition, seasoned somewhat by my personal Ceremonial and Qabalistic background, as the years progressed, interaction with other groups and traditions—Gardnerian, Alexandrian, Druidic, Celtic, and more—caused the First Temple of the Craft of W.I.C.A. to evolve into what it is today—a very eclectic coven.

Rituals used years ago have been rewritten again and again. New ideas, different concepts, and ways of working the Magick were introduced and either kept or rejected depending on their "feel" in Circle. As the Temple grew in knowledge and feeling, so did those who were a part of the Temple. Yet, a feeling also grew that we were erring in some way.

If you pick up almost any book concerning Witchcraft— from those written in the 60s and 70s to those written in the 90s—you will see reference after reference to one group or another's "Book of Shadows." The book that contains—for their eyes only—all of their rituals and teachings. Here and there in various books an author would print bits and pieces from some of the rituals done by the author's group, usually declaring that by publishing the information they were break- ing tradition at great personal risk. While these bits and pieces gave insight and feeling to what was being celebrated by the ritual, they did not provide enough information for people who were serious about Wicca as a religion and who were miles away from contact with a serious teacher or coven. These books did little to fully explain "or walk" a person through an entire ritual so that the individual might truly become one with that which was being ritually celebrated.

From its inception, the First Temple of the Craft of W.I.C.A. has believed in openness and sharing. Covens that joined with us to celebrate a change in the season were each given a copy of the ritual we used and told that they were welcome to use any or all of it in the future.

With the publication of my first book, *Turning of the Wheel*, rituals used by the First Temple of the Craft of W.I.C.A. to celebrate the Moons and the Festivals over the years were made available to everyone in the Pagan community to use and enjoy.

It is with that same intent of openness and sharing that I write this companion book. It, too, is a *Book of Shadows*. Within it are rituals used by the First Temple of the Craft of W.I.C.A. to celebrate both family and personal growth and initiation. I make this work available to the Wiccan/Pagan community to share that which has given special meaning through ritual to special times shared in love and knowledge. It is especially intended for those of you who, for whatever reason, do not have access to this kind of material so you can fully experience these ritual times. I ask that you feel free to use any or all of this work to add to your personal or your Coven's growth as you will and that you feel free to change parts or passages so that whatever you use will become yours and will grow with you.

I have been open about sharing information with you, and ask that you also be open and sharing with others who seek to work the path of Wicca.

May the Light of the Lord illume your path, and may the Love of the Lady be always in your heart.

Blessed Be!
Stanley J. A. Modrzyk, High Priest
First Temple of the Craft of W.I.C.A.

Acknowledgments

I give thanks for all those whose paths have interacted with mine, for with each interaction came knowledge—of them, of myself, and of our individual places within the Universe. Specifically, I would like to thank:

Fritz, whose wild unpredictability allowed me to see that letting go and being crazy IS okay.

Eli, whose unorthodox teachings opened my eyes to see the core of truth that underlies all beliefs.

Esther and Mike, students of mine, friends of mine, purveyors of simple beauty.

Introduction

For centuries books such as this one and my previous work, *Turning of the Wheel*, have been referred to as Books of Shadows. They are books containing the teachings and/or rituals of Covens within the Wiccan religion or Witchcraft which, because of religious and political persecutions of times past—and, in some cases, of times present—were kept hidden from sight, "in the shadows," so to speak, available only to members of the Coven.

This book and *Turning of the Wheel* are serious attempts to bring the rituals and the beliefs of Wicca out of the shadows and into the light where they belong, so that anyone—Wiccan or not—may be able to read, feel, and understand the meaning of Wicca, *the religion*. I hope that these books will not only allow those of Wicca to add to their knowledge and experience, but also dispel, through open enlightenment, some of the fear and negative myth that may dwell in the minds of those with other beliefs.

This Book of Shadows is broken down into three parts. In Part I, Background to Build On, I start with some of the beliefs of the Wiccan religion. While the beliefs discussed come from the First Temple of the Craft of W.I.C.A.'s eclectic tradition, these beliefs are, to some extent, shared by and common to most Wiccan groups.

Also in Part One I describe the altar setup and those ritual aspects that are common to most, if not all, of the rituals that follow in the book. By putting these common ritual elements together and explaining them once, I avoid repeating them over and over throughout the book.

In Part Two, Celebrating Family Times of Change, I discuss the meanings for Handfasting, Wiccaning, and Passing Over the Veil, and, for each of these times of change, give a complete ritual for you to use or draw from as you or your coven finds a need to celebrate one of these times.

Finally in Part Three, Celebrating Coven Times of Change, I discuss the temple makeup of the First Temple of the Craft of W.I.C.A. and the various rituals used to bring people into the coven and mark their growth and advancement once they are in the coven. Once again, for all but one of these times, complete rituals which can be used by anyone to mark these times are given.

Through openness and enlightenment, fear and misinformation can be done away with. By making the information in this book available, I hope to encourage that same desire for openness and awareness in others within the Wiccan community. I also hope that books like this one will further the open growth of Wicca in areas where, while people may feel a curiosity and even a need to know and learn of Wicca, there is no information readily available.

Years ago, a pagan magazine published by the late Herman Slater called the *Earth Religion News* had a motto on its cover page: "Guard the Mysteries—Reveal them constantly." It is in this same spirit that I urge you to read on— and share!

Note to the Reader

The reader is advised that the ways and teachings of Wicca are many and diverse. The beliefs, views, opinions, teachings, and rituals contained in this book are those of the First Temple of the Craft of W.I.C.A. and are not meant to be regarded as the "only way" or the "last word." While we feel that our teachings and rituals are sound, balanced, and fairly all-encompassing, as the saying goes, "there are many paths that lead to the top of the same mountain." Just because what you may read in this book is different from what you may read or be taught elsewhere does not make this book right or another wrong—only different. The only right or wrong among the many diverse paths of Wicca rests within you and how right or wrong they feel and work for you.

PART I

BASICS TO BUILD ON

From that which was, comes that which is,
    To bring forth what will be!
We all need basics to build on, to understand
    What we see.
For by knowing our roots and the strength of
the branch
    That we stand on,
We can fully perceive the Tree!

CHAPTER 1

WICCAN BELIEFS

WITCHCRAFT, WICCA, The Craft—different names for the same thing—Earth Religion. A religion that attempts to bring you into harmony with yourself and the forces within you as well as with all of nature and the forces of life outside you.

Within Wicca, as perception increases and you begin to experience the harmony that comes from knowing who you are and finding your place in the universe, instead of being pushed around by life you find yourself able to take charge and mold your life to your will. For all the myths that surround Wicca regarding potions, spells, and magickal doings, know that this self-awareness is the true magick of Wicca. The ability to bring yourself into balance and harmony with all that is life so that you may control the direction of your life with your will is the ultimate working of true Magick!

So, then, to be able to achieve this harmony and balance, what does Wicca believe and teach?

As with all religions, Wicca starts with a belief in a Supreme Being or Force. In Wicca, this entity may be referred to as the One, the Great Unmanifest, the Cosmic All, the Infinite, or any one of many other names. Wicca realizes, like all major religions, that finite beings like you and me cannot begin to comprehend the totality of the infinite concepts contained within the Great Unmanifest. Our minds have a limited ability and our language an even more limited ability to try and comprehend or relate to an infinite being. So, Wicca takes the Great Unmanifest, separates its basic polarities and brings them into relatable manifestation in the images and concepts of the God and the Goddess. Wicca further personalizes these manifestations of the Ultimate by referring to them as the Lord and the Lady. By using these images, Wicca gives us a godhead that we can relate to and identify with on a personal level.

The God represents the male potency of the universe portrayed in a variety of forms. At the Winter Solstice or Yule, He is the newborn Sun God. At the Summer Solstice, He is the mighty, radiant, all powerful Sun God. During the dark winter months, He may be called forth as the Horned God, the God of the Hunt. At Samhain—the death festival—He is the Lord of Death and Resurrection. In each instance He is the male potency of the universe varying only in the particular aspect needing prominence because of the time of the year. All in all, He is STRENGTH, INTELLECT, LOGIC. He is the FORCE that gives all LIFE!

In the Wiccan religion, acknowledging the God and coming to know His attributes and identifying with Him brings men closer to their masculine abilities and power. It also emphasizes the responsibilities that come with these abilities. For women, the ability to identify with the God brings growth as they come to realize their masculine side and the strength, logic, and power they may never have been aware of within them.

The Goddess represents the female potency of the universe and is also portrayed in a variety of forms. At the New Moon, She is the Promise Reborn. At the Full Moon, She is the Radiant Mother. In the springtime, She is the young Maiden, virginal, and full of curiosity, waiting to explore life. By Samhain, in late fall, She is the withered Crone fully knowledgeable of life having passed through all of its seasons. At each of these times She is the female potency of the universe varying only in the aspect needing prominence because of the time of the year. All in all She is EMOTION, INTUITION, FEELING. She is the power that gives the life force FORM.

In the Wiccan religion, acknowledging the Goddess and coming to know Her attributes and identifying with Her brings women closer to their feminine abilities and intuition. It also emphasizes the responsibilities that come with them. For men, the ability to identify with the Goddess brings growth as they come to realize their feminine side and come to feel the emotion and intuition they may have never been aware of within them.

It is important to remember that the God and the Goddess are the two polarities of the whole, and attentive worship of either one without the inclusion of the other creates instability. Likewise, within ourselves as the microcosm, we are the whole and, regardless of gender, to attune to either polarity—God or Goddess—without balancing ourselves by accepting and understanding its mate, results in an unstable existence that will never really achieve its full potential. Each aspect, though self-creating and self-sustaining, is impotent without its balance in the other. Both the God and the Goddess—without and within—are needed if life and growth are to be.

To help bring people into awareness and balance by getting to know the God and the Goddess, the Wiccan religion celebrates two cycles that constantly occur in nature.

First, on a close personal level, in touch especially with the female flow and cycle, the Wiccan religion follows the lunar cycle and celebrates both its beginning with the observance of the New Moon's first light and its fulfillment with the celebration of the Full Moon in all its radiance. As the moon in the sky grows from the Lady's first crescent promise to Her complete full radiance, so, too, do we feel the growth in our emotions and how this change affects our balance. The cycle is one of waxing growth and increase to overflowing completion, and then one of a waning energy flowing back to nothingness awaiting the cycle to begin again.

At the cycle's beginning, we celebrate the New Moon's first crescent. It is a time to feel the renewal and rededicate one's self to growth and enlightenment. It is a time for new beginnings and a time to work magick for positive increases in whatever areas in life that need advancement.

With the Full Moon, and its inspiring beauty, we gather to celebrate and share the emotional completeness this time can bring. We share the elements to bring ourselves into balance with nature and fulfill our potential. It is a time of deep feeling and rich emotion. From this time forward, the cycle is now one of decreasing energy with the Lady's light lessening in the sky each night until it disappears altogether while we work magick for the decrease or elimination of things that are negative in our life.

As the Wiccan religion seeks to become one with these times and work with the flow of the energy under the light and power of the Goddess, we also seek to keep our balance; so, as we celebrate under the Lady's light and are moved by the energy we feel, we also bring forth the Lord, for without the light of the Sun God the Lady would be dark, empty, and unknown to us. The Lord gives the Lady the energy to shine forth in the evening sky and the Lady allows the otherwise blinding and unperceivable brilliance of the Lord to be realized through Her.

On a larger scale, knowledge of and balance with the God and the Goddess is gained in the Wiccan religion through the annual cycle celebrating the turning of the Wheel of Life. With its eight season-changing festivals, the Wheel of Life is a complete celebration of all that is life running its complete cycle from birth through death—and, of course, rebirth. Within these eight season-changing festivals, four are related directly to the Sun's progression throughout the year and are known as Solar festivals. The other four festivals occur approximately midpoint between the Solar festivals and, so, are known as Cross festivals. While the Solar festivals denote a particular point in the Sun's annual passing and are directly related to the Sun God and the Cross festivals are more directly related to specific occurrences pertaining to the Earth's cycles and the Goddess, each of the festivals is a time to bring forth both the God and the Goddess equally. Balance is the way of Wicca. At every festival there are aspects of both the God and the Goddess to perceive and celebrate. Force and Form at each of these times marks the movement of the Wheel of Life that we need to be aware of and grow with. As mentioned, each of the eight festivals marks a specific time in the life cycle beginning with birth and proceeding through the cycle to death. In Wicca, we gather at these times so that we may become one with the energies within the life cycle, know them, and by so knowing lend our energy to the continued turning of the Wheel of Life.

The Festivals

For those who are not familiar with the festivals celebrated by Wicca, they are (in the order celebrated by the First Temple of the Craft of W.I.C.A.):

1. *Winter Solstice*—also known as Yule and celebrated around December 21, the Winter Solstice is the shortest day of the year. For months the days have grown shorter and shorter as the Sun God has faded away. With the coming dawn, the Sun God will be reborn of Himself and grow stronger with each passing day bringing back light and life-giving energy to the Earth. It is a birth celebration! Yet, while the Winter Solstice centers around the young Sun God's rebirth, the time is still one of inner reflection presided over by the Crone aspect of the Triple Goddess.

2. *Imbolc*—also known as Candlemas, Imbolc is celebrated on February 2. The time is midpoint between the rebirth of the Sun God at the Winter Solstice and the return of the Goddess from the Underworld as the youthful Maiden at the Spring Equinox. Imbolc is a celebration where we use candles to symbolically give strength to the young Sun God's continued growth as well as light the way for the Goddess' return from the darkness of the Underworld. As the Winter Solstice is a celebration of birth, Imbolc is a celebration giving guidance and direction to the youthful God and Goddess as they grow toward puberty.

3. *Spring Equinox*—celebrated around March 21, is a day when light and dark are equal. However, from this time forward light will triumph over darkness and the night will be rolled back. The Sun God has come of age and will rule. By coming of age, the Sun God has brought warmth and life back

to the earth. The winds now blow from the south bringing warmth. Animals long in hibernation begin to awake. The trees begin to reawaken as they show forth new buds. All in all there is a renewal of life upon the earth to welcome back the Goddess from the Underworld. Spring Equinox is Her time as well. Going down into the Underworld as the withered Crone at Samhain, She has now come back to us as Core, the young, virginal Maiden. Spring Equinox celebrates the youthful innocence of life renewed and joyful.

4. *Beltane*—or May Day's eve is celebrated April 30 by many groups as well as the First Temple. Because of the many varied traditions within Wicca, many groups will celebrate Beltane on May 1 as May Day. Whether celebrated the evening of April 30 or under the bright May sun on May 1, Beltane is a festival celebrating fertility. The earth, warmed by the sun has been turned and the fields are ready for impregnation with the waiting seeds. The evening festival is usually marked by the lighting of the bale fires to burn away the dross of winter and to purify the land, humankind, and beast. The May Day festival is marked by that great phallic symbol—the May Pole. At either celebration, in days of old, people would go into the fields leaping high with broomsticks—bristle end up—to show how high the fertile crops would grow. (For some crops the hole made with the handle end as the people came down was filled with seeds being planted by others following.)

5. *Summer Solstice*—also known as High Summer, is celebrated around June 20. The Summer Solstice is the longest day of the year. The Sun God reigns supreme. Yet for all His power, with sunset this day His power will begin to diminish. We gather to do honor to the life-force of the Sun God which manifests around us in the bounty brought forth upon the earth. For that bounty all around us, we also gather to give thanks to the Earth Mother overflowing in Her pregnant beauty. Flowers of every color and hue can be seen wherever we look. Beginning fruits on tree and vine give promise of the

generous harvest that She will graciously give to us in fall. The Summer Solstice is the union of the powerful God and the pregnant Goddess and we are the celebrants at this magnificent summer reception. In many cultures a marriage was not considered valid until the wife could show evidence that she was fertile and could produce offspring. Hence, here we have the Goddess—in the form of the Earth Mother—in Her radiant pregnant beauty joining in formal union (marriage) with the God. While Beltane celebrated the fertile coupling of the God and the Goddess, the Summer Solstice celebrates their actual marriage. This is also why June has always been considered the month for weddings.

6. *Lammas*—celebrated on August 1, marks the beginning of maturity as this is the festival that celebrates the beginning of the harvest. The first fruits have been brought in and if we take time to look we can see the bounty of the harvest that still lies before us. The bounty of the Earth Mother we have tended is now in our care to bring in and store in preparation for the months ahead.

7. *Fall Equinox*—is celebrated around September 21. Once again day and night are equal and in balance. But, with sunset this day, night and darkness will triumph as the Sun God slowly dies and yields His rule to the Dark Lord of the Hunt, the Lord of Death and Resurrection. It is at this time that we give thanks and bid farewell to the Sun God. This time also marks the completion of the harvest. The harvest from Lammas until now has been weeks of hard work. Now we see the storehouse near to full and we break to relax and celebrate. With a few exceptions, the harvest is in and it is now a time to give thanks to the Earth Mother for Her bounty shared with us.

8. *Samhain*—also known as Halloween, is celebrated on October 31. Samhain is the Death Festival. As we look around us, we see that the grass is no longer green and full of life. The winds have shifted and now blow from the north with an icy

chill. In the fields, the flowers are gone. The harvest is in, and all that remains are lifeless stalks and husks. This is a time when the earth has come full cycle and is dying. Yet, with death comes life, for from the fruits harvested in fall will come the seeds of new life for planting in the spring. Without death, life would not continue. Marking the beginning of a time for introspection, Samhain moves the Wheel of Life the final turn to complete the cycle of life from birth through to death.[1]

The Elements

Another belief within the Wiccan religion is that all life is comprised of five elemental aspects: Spirit, Air, Fire, Water, and Earth. In Wicca they are referred to as the Elements or the Mighty Forces.

Spirit is the ever present personal energy that binds the other four elements together into a cohesive whole. Depending on the culture, the Spirit element may be called the Self, the Ba, or the Soul. The Spirit element is the essence that makes each of us who we should be if we would but follow our inner divine will.

The Spirit element, because it is so personal and indistinct, is not usually represented on the altar in a Wiccan circle. Each of the other four elements as they are more definable will usually be represented on the altar in a Wiccan circle and be assigned to one of the four cardinal directions. Each of the remaining four elements will also have a specific color and, for invocation, a specific name—usually that of a God, Goddess, Archangel, or mythical figure. Because of the many varying traditions within Wicca, the particular color and name association may be different from group to group.

---

[1] For a more detailed explanation of these times that mark the turning of the Wheel of Life and complete rituals for their celebration, see my book *Turning of the Wheel* (York Beach, ME: Samuel Weiser, 1993).

The elemental aspect of Air represents pure conceptual thought, the first glimmer of an idea. Nothing can exist without being thought of first. In the circle, we assign the element of Air to the East and give it the color yellow. On the altar, the element of Air is symbolized by the incense burned on the censer. To summon the element of Air, we call to the Archangel Raphael. The symbolic being of Air is the Sylph.

The elemental aspect of Fire represents the life force in all things. We say that our bodies "burn calories" when we work and play. When we see young athletes succeeding we say that they are full of the "fire of life." Life is a process of combustion—fire. We assign Fire to the south and give it the color red. On the altar the element of Fire is symbolized by the red fire candle. To summon forth the element of Fire we call upon the archangel Michael. The symbolic being of fire is the Salamander.

The elemental aspect of Water represents the emotional fluidity of nature. In all things there is the element of Water. The human body is about 80% water; so just as the oceans have tides, we, too, are affected by pulls and currents. Similarly, our emotional ups and downs create pulls on the emotional currents of others—another example of the element of Water in action. We assign the element of Water to the west and give it the color blue. On the altar the element of Water is symbolized by a dish or bowl of rain water into which has been placed some seashells and some clear quartz crystals. To summon forth the element of Water we call upon the archangel Gabriel. The symbolic being of Water is the Undine.

The elemental aspect of Earth represents the material manifested plane of existence. The element of Earth is the here and now. It is the manifested end result occurring after conceptual thought (Air) has been given life (Fire) and the emotion to flow (Water) into being (Earth). We assign the element of Earth to the north and give it the color green. On the altar the element of Earth is symbolized by a dish of either real earth or sea salt to which has been added several stones. To summon forth the element of Earth we call upon the archangel Uriel. The symbolic being for Earth is the Gnome.

Each of us at any given moment contains all of the elements in various ratios. Sometimes these ratios can go to extremes and be detrimental to our wellbeing. Wicca, as a religion, uses various exercises and ritual celebrations to get members to realize these elemental energies within themselves and then bring these energies into balance and harmony. By bringing the elemental energies into balance within, you find a greater awareness of your total being and a closer harmony with all of nature—including the other people that are close to you. Nobody exists in perfect balance at all times. Wicca tries to give you the means to come into contact with yourself, allowing you to find the elemental balance necessary to move forward on your path and grow.

To bring energy and meaning to the rituals we do today, the Wiccan religion draws upon the various mythologies of the past. Which particular mythos a group will use depends upon the tradition the group is following or the background of the group's leaders. A group may orient their rituals according to Egyptian, Greek, Norse, or even American Indian mythology to bring the energy of the past forth to give the rituals intent. In some instances a group will draw on more than one mythology for meaning in their rituals. Again, because of the varied traditions within the Wiccan religion, we will find diversity; but it does not matter as to the specific mythology utilized by a group. It only matters that the particular mythology is seriously taught to the group and understood by the people in the group so that they may seriously relate to the meanings portrayed through the rituals. All mythologies focus on the same central themes and give insight into the mysteries of Nature. When a group uses a particular mythos to bring meaning to a ritual, the group has made that ritual a true life experience.

Basically the rituals done in Wicca can be broken down into three types or groups of rituals.

First there are the rituals used to celebrate the seasonal changes marked by the Turning of the Wheel of Life and the flow of the Lunar cycle. These are serious religious observances. They mark the times when we seek to achieve identity and balance with the God and the Goddess and all that is in nature. These rituals are used to bring us closer to the flow of life so that we may move with it rather than against it. Examples of this first group of rituals and their meanings are covered in my book *Turning of the Wheel*.

Second, there are the rituals of family bonding and growth that are used to mark and celebrate a particular time on the personal family level. The Handfasting or marriage rite which marks the beginning for a couple as a family is one such ritual. After the couple has a child, the Wiccaning for that child—similar to a Christening—is another such ritual. Lastly, the rite for Passing Beyond the Veil done for those who have left this plane of existence for a while is a personal family ritual. In each of these times the God and the Goddess are called upon to witness and give special blessings to those people involved. In each of these times special energies are directed to the family celebrating the ritual.

Third, there are the rituals that mark a specific point of personal growth or achievement, usually within a coven. These are the initiatory rites set up within the coven. Different groups may use a different number of levels of initiations and may call them by different names. In the First Temple of the Craft of W.I.C.A. these levels and their attending rituals are Affirmation, Dedication, First Degree Initiation, and Second Degree Initiation. Affirmation marks the time when a newcomer has learned enough about the Wiccan religion to publicly affirm that this is a comfortable path for her or him. Dedication marks the time when a student formally decides that the Wiccan religion will be his or her path. First Degree and Second Degree initiations mark levels of achievement and balance attained as the individual practices and grows within the Wiccan religion.

The last two groups of rituals are explained in this Book of Shadows. Complete rituals with which to celebrate these times (except Second Degree Initiation) are included.

To conclude, then, what are the beliefs of Wicca?

○ Wicca does believe in a Supreme Being.

○ Wicca identifies with the male and female aspects of this Supreme Being as contained in the personae of the God and the Goddess.

○ Wicca believes that life is a balanced ratio of five elements within all and that the goal of life is to achieve that balance daily.

○ Wicca believes that by celebrating the New Moon and the Full Moon aspects of the lunar cycle we can open ourselves to the personal flow of life and harmony that they signify.

○ Wicca believes that by celebrating the eight times marked on the Wheel of Life we can tune our energies to the changes in the earth around us and bring ourselves into harmony with the earth and its annual rhythm.

By so doing we bring real Magick into our lives!

So Mote It Be!

CHAPTER 2

COMMON
RITUAL ELEMENTS

WITHIN THE Wiccan religion there are a multitude of various traditions or backgrounds. Gardnerian Wicca, Seax-Wica, Druidic Craft, Pagan Way, and Celtic Wicca are but a few of the different "mainstream" traditions. Each of these traditions covers a variety of groups that each vary slightly (or more than slightly) from each other depending upon, among other things, the group's location and the group's specific founder or teacher. There are also numerous "family" traditions and groups, like the First Temple of the Craft of W.I.C.A., that began with a core of teaching from one of the mainline traditions and, through open interaction with other groups, incorporated new ways and teachings over time and evolved into a new eclectic tradition.

Regardless of the background or tradition, within the Wiccan religion all groups share the same basic beliefs and celebrate or acknowledge the same times marked on the Wheel of Life and those times marking the Lunar cycle. Because of this, no matter how diverse their individual rituals may be, all of their rituals will contain common elements that will allow people from one group to participate with understanding in the rituals of another group with little additional training and explanation. For a particular group these common ritual elements will usually be done in a nearly identical manner in all their rituals.

The following common ritual elements are used in most of the rituals performed in the First Temple of the Craft of W. I. C. A.

The Circle

The Wiccan religion does not require a large physical edifice (such as a church building) to hold or contain sacred space to worship or do ritual work, for all space on Earth is sacred to those within the Wiccan religion. All that is needed in Wicca is a means to set a particular spot apart from the rest of creation to insulate it from distractions and any negative energy that might be around. To accomplish this, most Wiccans cast a Circle of Protection around a central working area. By casting this Circle, Wiccans set up a sacred space that exists apart from "mundane" reality. This becomes a space outside of time where unlimited energy can be raised and directed. The Circle[1] becomes the Wiccan Temple wherein the Goddess and the God can be called forth and worshiped. Within the Circle, chant, song, and dance are used to raise energy and bring all together as one—with each other, with the Goddess, the God, and the forces invoked to presence.

While the Circle is intended for use in carving a sacred niche out of the living room, basement recreation room, or other mundane setting where a temple area is needed, some groups who use the outdoors for their ritual area will also cast a formal Circle to make their ritual space that much more special and set apart from everyday reality. Their space will be apart from and outside of Nature and, yet, still one with Nature and even closer to its true essence.

Casting a Circle can be a simple mental exercise or an extremely ceremonial physical exercise depending on several factors, including the preference of the individual or group, the background of the individual or tradition of the group, and the nature of any work to be done in the Circle. With time and training, an individual can cast a Circle for a private, yet extremely complex, magickal working without even leaving his or her easy chair.

---

[1] The term Circle is somewhat misleading. What is actually being set up is a sphere, like a large bubble, that extends not only around the area, but above and below the area as well.

A simple Circle casting for a solitary Wiccan has the person stand in the center of what will become the Circle space, extend an arm out front with the forefinger (or if the person has one, the athame) pointed to the floor area where the Circle will be laid down and slowly turn clockwise (to the right). While turning, he or she visualizes a veil of light blue flame springing up from the floor just beyond the fingertips and chants:

A place outside of space and time. A sacred space that's safe, that's MINE!

Once the rotation is complete, the Circle has been formed.

The starting point of a Circle will depend on the background or tradition of the individual or group. While the First Temple of the Craft of W.I.C.A. uses an East/West axis in our circles with the starting point in the east for our rituals, there are some groups that use a North/South axis in their circles and begin their rituals in the North. Reasons can be advanced for either alignment—each group follows the orientation it was taught and that feels comfortable for the group.

As to the size of the Circle, while most books written describe or recommend a circle with a nine-foot diameter, in the real world most people would be hard pressed to find a room in their house or apartment large enough and clear enough to cast a nine-foot diameter Circle. What matters most about the size is that the Circle cast is large enough for those inside to be able to move and be comfortable. As long as this is accomplished, the energy can be raised and can flow without interference or tension.

The Altar

The Circle creates the sacred space for the person or group to work in. Inside the Circle the group will usually set up an altar. The altar acts as both a surface to work on and a focal point for concentration to center the energy raised in some workings.

Figure 1. Basic Ritual Altar set up. You are looking at the altar from where the Priest and Priestess would stand. To your left (North) is a bowl containing sea salt and some stones representing the element Earth. Directly before you (West) is a bowl with rain water and a sea shell representing the element Water. To your right (South) is a red candle that represents the element Fire. Directly across the altar from you (East) is the censer with a piece of charcoal in it. To the left of the censer is a piece of parchment with loose incense on it. Behind the censer is the ceremonial sword for casting the Circle. On either side of the censer are the altar candles. Before you, on either side of the water dish, are reading candles used by the Priest and Priestess to give light to any script they may need to read.

The orientation of the altar will usually coincide with the group's orientation regarding the circle's starting point. That is, for groups (like the First Temple of the Craft of W.I.C.A.), oriented on an East/West axis, the front of the altar will be its east side and the Priest and the Priestess will work from the west side of the altar facing east. For groups that are oriented on a North/South axis, the front of the altar will be its north side, with the Priest and Priestess working in the south facing north.

The altar can be made of almost any material that the individual or group is comfortable with. Its shape can be circular, square, or rectangular—whatever shape the group feels is right for its members. What does matter is the size of the altar's surface, and its height. The top surface needs to be large enough to comfortably hold all the items necessary for the ritual. Ritual concentration is hard to hold if to pick up the ceremonial sword you first have to move the censer and the fire candle. The altar should be high enough for the Priest and the Priestess to work from comfortably without developing back strain from bending.

The temple altar used by the First Temple of the Craft of W.I.C.A. is a large tree trunk section[2] about two feet high topped with a small rectangular table flat. The Temple hopes to replace the table flat with a piece of black marble in the near future.

For rituals, the altar is covered with an altar cloth of an appropriate color. When celebrating the moons, the Temple uses a black altar cloth. For the various festivals, the altar cloth will be of a color or colors that pertains to the season being celebrated.

The basic altar set up starts with two white altar candles, primarily for illumination, one in the northeast corner and one in the southeast corner of the altar. Centered on each of the four sides are the elemental representations. On the east side is a censer with charcoal for burning incense to represent Air.

---

[2] The tree trunk section we use came from a tree that was cut down because it died. There was no needless sacrifice of the living.

On the south side is a red candle to represent Fire. On the west side is a bowl of rain water to represent Water. Finally, on the north side is a dish of sea salt to represent Earth.

The ceremonial sword used by the Temple for casting the Circle is placed along the eastern edge of the altar with the hilt to the south. Reading candles—used for close illumination—for the Priest and the Priestess as well as the athames of the Priest and the Priestess are also on the altar.

Although other items, such as a chalice, pentacle, cakes, or wine may be placed upon the altar for particular rituals, this is the basic common altar set up used by the First Temple of the Craft of W.I.C.A. in the rituals described in this book. (See figure 1 on page 18.)

Full Formal Circle Casting

While the short and simple circle casting given earlier will work great for a personal ritual, for a large formal gathering a full elemental fivefold circle casting is usually done by the Temple.

To start, the Priest will cleanse the Earth element by doing a solar cross with his athame over the element three times while saying:

"I exorcise thee, O element of Earth, casting out all impurities that might lie within."

As he finishes, he plunges his athame into the dish of salt, feeling a bolt of energy blasting away any negativity that might have been there.

Then, the Priest repeats these actions with the Water element while saying:

"I exorcise thee, O element of Water, casting out all impurities that might lie within."

When he finishes, he mixes three pinches of the Earth element into the Water element and hands the bowl to the

Priestess who walks the Circle clockwise from the east aspersing the Circle and those within it as she goes around. By doing so, the Priestess—using the combined elements of Earth and Water—casts at once the first two elemental circles, Earth and Water.

As the Priestess returns to the east, the Priest adds incense to the censer. Then as the Priestess returns to the altar, the Priest picks up the censer and goes to the east. From there he walks the Circle clockwise pausing to cense each of the four quarter points—East, South, West, and North, in turn. When he has finished the circle, and returned to the East, he turns to face the altar and does an Earth banishing pentagram with the censer as he says:

"With Fire and Air do I banish all negative force and feeling from within this sacred space."

The Priest has now—using the combined elements of Fire and Air—cast at once the second two elemental circles, Fire and Air.

The Priest returns to the east side of the altar, puts the censer back, picks up the ceremonial sword and hands the sword hilt first across the altar to the Priestess. This is the symbolic channeling of the Lord's power to the Lady to use as she wills. Throughout the ritual it is the function of the Priestess to take the energy raised and give it direction and form.

The Priestess takes the ceremonial sword, and starting in the east, formally casts the Circle by walking its circumference clockwise while chanting:

"I conjure thee, O Circle of power, that thou be-est as a boundary between the worlds of men and the realms of the Mighty Ones! A guardian and a protection to preserve and contain the power that we shall raise within. Therefore do I bless and consecrate thee. So mote it be!"

As she walks she visualizes a blue flame springing up just beyond the sword's point creating a veil of blue flame/fire.

Everyone in the Circle responds:

"So mote it be!"

The Priestess then replaces the ceremonial sword on the east-ern edge of the altar. The Priestess has just cast the Circle with the fifth element, Spirit—the element that binds together the other four elements, to truly create an area outside of space and time.

Just as it is necessary to cast the Circle to create a space to do the ritual outside of traditional reality, once the ritual is complete it is necessary to uncast the Circle to reopen the space and bring it back into focus with traditional reality.

To do this, the Priestess takes the ceremonial sword from the altar, goes to the east, and walks the circumference of the circle *counterclockwise*, visualizing the veil of blue flame fad-ing and vanishing as she walks by. Once she has walked full circle back to the east, she turns to face the group and, hold-ing the sword point down before her says:

"The Circle is open, yet unbroken! So mote it be!"

Everyone responds: **"So mote it be!"**

The Aura and its Opening

Around each of us is a personal energy field known as the aura. This personal energy field is maintained by a semiper-meable barrier called the auric shield. From day to day in life, the auric shield protects us by deflecting the bulk of any massive bursts of psychic energy we might encounter— either positive or negative. It protects us from having our energy drained by a psychic vampire, should we encounter one, or by a seriously ill relative or friend.

For example, you may have experienced walking into a hospital room of a critically ill person, and while feeling fine up to this time, you suddenly find yourself feeling weak or "down." You may have had an intense desire to leave the room as soon as possible. This desire became stronger the longer you stayed in the room! The feeling was real. The seriously—possibly terminally—ill person was in dire need of whatever life energy you could provide. The patient's void or negative energy field was feeding on your positively charged field and was pulling/draining your life energy. The longer you stayed, the more your life energy was drained until you were forced to leave. While your auric shield prevents a serious energy drain early in such encounters, as the drain continues, it sets off alarms generating a repulsion to the pull, creating a real need to leave to keep you safe.

We feel positive or negative influences and the energy drains like the one described because the auric shield does allow for some seepage to occur. However, we are not usually overwhelmed or subject to harm by a high positive or negative energy field unless we ourselves are ill, weak, or have deliberately opened our auric shield to such influence.

Because of the auric shield, if energy is to be raised, shared, or used in a ritual, each person in the ritual must consciously open his or her auric shield. For some people who have background and experience, opening their auric shields may only require a moment of meditative silence. Most people, however, require a conscious aura opening exercise in order to open or close their auric shields. One of the best aura opening exercises you can use for this purpose and one that the First Temple of the Craft of W.I.C.A. has used and taught for over twenty years is the Qabalistic Cross.

There are several reasons why the Qabalistic Cross is an excellent exercise for opening the auric shield prior to beginning work in a circle. First, the Qabalistic Cross exercise sets a frame of mind by bringing to consciousness the divinity within each of us, forming a link with the energy of the Universe. Secondly, by performing the Qabalistic Cross exercise energy channels within and around us are opened and, if needed, renewed so that we begin the ritual more aware. Finally, the Qabalistic Cross exercise, when so used, opens the self to all the energies that will be brought in and raised in Circle during the ritual.

While the Qabalistic Cross exercise has appeared in numerous books throughout the years, a full explanation of its uses was rare. Because of this, in part, people tended to consider the Qabalistic Cross exercise as something that was strictly a part of and only done for Ceremonial Magick.

For those who are unfamiliar with the Qabalistic Cross exercise, here it is as taught by the First Temple of the Craft of W.I.C.A.

The Qabalistic Cross

Once the Circle has been fully cast, stand facing the east quarter. (If you are doing this exercise with a group, all stand facing East and perform the following motions in unison.) Raise your right hand to a point just over your forehead. Slowly bring your hand down in front of you to your solar plexus as you chant:

"Ateh" (Ah-teh), which means "Thou Art."

As you are bringing your hand down, visualize a shaft of radiant energy coming down from above and traveling through your being to your solar plexus.[3]

Next move your hand down in front of you toward the ground and feel the energy of the Earth. Slowly bring your hand up to your solar plexus bringing with it a second shaft of radiant energy up from the Earth, through you to join with the first shaft of energy at your solar plexus. As you do this, chant:

"Malkuth" (mal-kuth), which means "The Kingdom."

---

[3] In doing the visualization for the Qabalistic Cross exercise there are some people who have difficulty visualizing the shaft of radiant energy flowing through themselves. Instead, they see themselves "standing" in front of themselves and the energy flowing through this image. Nothing wrong with this, do what is comfortable for you.

Now extend your right hand straight out to your right. As you chant:

"Ve Geburah" (veh-geh-bur-ah), which means "The Power,"

bring your hand in toward your solar plexus visualizing a shaft of radiant energy coming in from the right to meet and join with the other three already formed.

Next extend your right hand straight out to the left. Slowly bring it back to your solar plexus bringing with it a fourth shaft of radiant energy to join with the others. As you do this, chant:

"Ve Gedulah" (veh-geh-du-lah), which means "The Glory."

At this point, with hands clasped (as in prayer) or with arms folded over each other in the Osiris position, slowly unfold your arms and open your hands until they are stretched out wide.[4] While you are doing this visualize and feel your auric shield opening, like the opening of closed drapes. As you do this, chant:

"Le Olahm" (leh-o-lam), which means "Unto All Things, Unto All Times."

Finally, as you stand open, chant:

"Amen" (ah-mmm-eh-nnn),

sounding each letter distinctly. Your auric shield is now open and you are fully able to use/draw/send the energies as they may be raised within the Circle.

---

[4] For those of you unfamiliar with the Osiris position, stand straight with your arms crossed over your chest—left arm over right—in such a way that your right thumb touches the left side of your neck and your left thumb touches the right side of your neck. This position is also called the Osiris Risen position.

The words you chanted to open yourself translate as "Thou art the Kingdom, the Power, the Glory, unto all things, unto all times, Amen." It is important to remember that the opening "Thou" refers to the Godhead without and the self within simultaneously. It is your personal affirmation and realization of the Godhood that exists within you. Believe it!

Just as the Qabalistic Cross exercise is used to open the auric shield, it is also used to close the auric shield once the ritual is over but before the Circle is uncast. To close your auric shield, do the Qabalistic Cross exercise just as you did for opening the shield, except after chanting "Ve Gedulah," instead of clasping your hands and folding your arms, start with your hands open and your arms stretched out. Then, as you chant "Le Olahm," slowly bring your arms together and close your hands and your auric shield. As you are doing this, feel the positive energies raised during the ritual drawn into your aura and held there.

If for any reason you would leave the protective space created by the Circle without first closing your auric shield, do not worry. The natural state for your auric shield is a closed position. As such, it will close itself naturally once you return to the everyday world. It will re-establish itself more quickly if there is some threat to your personal energy level. Though you might lose some energy (both ritual and personal) while your auric shield remains open, most celebrations and rituals raise so much energy that you will have an excess and a minor loss will be nothing to worry about. If you find yourself halfway home and realize that you have not closed your auric shield, you can simply form a closed mental Circle and go through the closing ritual in your mind. Not noticing that your auric shield is still open is a good indication that whatever ritual you participated in raised so much good energy that you had an overflow.

In addition to opening and closing the auric shield, the Qabalistic Cross exercise has one other application. It can be used to measure your particular state of balance at any given moment in time. The exercise is done without opening the aura. Your attention is given to the point where the various radiant shafts of energy converge. They should come together at your solar plexus. If the vertical shaft joins well below the solar plexus, your head is in the clouds so you need some grounding. Conversely, if the shaft of energy coming from the Earth center is so strong as to force the center point farther up, you are too "earthy" and need to spend more time on spiritual things. As for the horizontal shaft, if it meets toward the left of center you need to quell some anger and be more giving. If the meeting point is to the right of center, you need to be more assertive and less giving—before you give everything away.

Invoking the Forces

The Circle has been cast and the auras have been opened. Now it is time to invoke the elemental forces to presence. In the previous chapter the elemental forces—Air, Fire, Water, and Earth—were introduced along with their alignments with each of the four cardinal directions and some of the names/forms used by the First Temple of the Craft of W.I.C.A. and other groups to call them forth.

Some Wiccan groups, like the First Temple of the Craft of W.I.C.A., call to them first as the Mighty Forces and, then, with the invocation specifically by name, i.e., Raphael, Michael, Gabriel, Uriel. Other groups may refer to them as the Guardians of the Elements or the Kings of the Elements or the Mighty Ones of the Four Quarters and, then, not name them or use Celtic or Norse specific names. Still other groups after the initial invocation may call to them in their forms of Sylph, Salamander, Undine, and Gnome. The important thing here is to know and understand the nature of the forces being invoked and the specific type of energy each one brings into the Circle.

The following examples are the invocations used most frequently by the First Temple of the Craft of W.I.C.A. The actions described are done with the Priest leading and the rest of the coven following in unison if it is a full coven doing the ritual, or performed by the individual if it is a solitary ritual.

Beginning in the east facing out of the circle with your right hand or athame in your right hand extended before you say:

"Mighty Forces of the East, we/I invoke and invite you to attend this rite and to guard this Circle."

Next you make an Air invoking pentagram[5] before you. Upon completing the pentagram, take your hand or athame, pierce the center of the pentagram creating a doorway and chant **"Raphael."** As you are chanting the name, visualize Raphael before you in flowing, airy, yellow robes and bring the Air element into the Circle as you bring your hand or athame in toward you. Briefly touch your forehead saying:

"One in mind"

and, then, touch your solar plexus saying:

"One in spirit".

This action reaffirms that as you bring the element to presence around and within you, you are working through your mind and your heart within the Circle.

The invocation is repeated as you move to each of the other quarters in turn, with the appropriate sign made for each of the other elements.

In the South, the invocation begins **"Mighty Forces of the South. . . ."** and the name chanted is **"Michael."** The pentagram used is Fire invoking and the figure appears in fiery red robes.

---

[5] For those unfamiliar with how to do the specific elemental invoking and dismissing pentagrams, there are how-to instructions given in the Glossary and in other books, including Aleister Crowley's *Magick in Theory and Practice*. Several editions of this work have been published. Samuel Weiser published the newest annotated version of Crowley's *Magick*, edited by the Ordo Templi Orientis, in 1994.

In the West, the invocation begins **"Mighty Forces of the West. . . ."** and the name chanted is **"Gabriel."** The pentagram used is Water invoking and the figure appears in watery aqua-blue robes.

In the North, the invocation begins **"Mighty Forces of the North. . . ."** and the name chanted is **"Uriel."** The pentagram used is Earth invoking[6] and the figure appears in forest green robes.

Once the ritual is complete, the forces invoked at the beginning need to be dismissed. The First Temple of the Craft of W.I.C.A. uses the following elemental dismissals. The Priestess performs the dismissals with the rest of the coven following in unison. For a solitary ritual, the dismissals are performed as shown by the individual.

Elemental Dismissals

Beginning in the East facing out of the circle, with your hand/athame extended before you, say:

"Mighty Forces of the East, we/I thank you for attending, but, if go you must, we/I say, Hail"—bring your hand back, kiss your wrist lightly and re-extend your hand/athame keeping your palm facing up[7]—**"and, Farewell!"**

Then do an Air dismissing pentagram.

Proceed, to each of the other three quarters repeating this dismissal at each quarter substituting the appropriate direction and elemental dismissing pentagram.

---

[6] There are groups that use the Earth invoking and dismissing pentagrams for all of the quarters rather than the specific elemental pentagrams. If you are visiting with another group, watch how the first (East) pentagram is done and then "go with the flow."

[7] Long ago when the blade was *the* weapon of choice, wounds to the wrist were dooming injuries that left people defenseless and open to death. Therfore, to extend a hand with the wrist exposed and open to injury was an ultimate sign of trust and goodwill.

For example in the South, the dismissal begins **"Mighty Forces of the South. . ."** and you do a Fire dismissing pentagram. In the West, the dismissal begins **"Mighty Forces of the West. . ."** and you do a Water dismissing pentagram. In the North, the dismissal begins **"Mighty Forces of the North. . ."** and you do an Earth dismissing pentagram.

At each quarter, the power of the Circle is enhanced by the presence of the particular elemental so the dismissals should be done in thankful reverence. The presence of the elements should "feel" gone, yet the power of each element should still be felt within.

Invoking the God and the Goddess

For most rituals, once the Forces have been invoked to presence, the next step is invoking the God and the Goddess. In the First Temple of the Craft of W.I.C.A. there are two main ways of bringing forth the God and the Goddess.

The first way, used at the New Moon and most other rituals, begins as the Priest goes to the east after he has finished the elemental invocations and faces out of the circle. He does an invoking hexagram and says:

"Hear me, O Ancient One! Mighty Cernunnos! Ra! Lord of Death and Resurrection! Consort of the Lady! We invoke and call upon thee. Be one with us and within us here in this, Thy sacred place. May the magick that we do be aided by Thy powers—the powers of Life that were, that are, that shall ever be! So mote it be!"

Everyone repeats: **"So mote it be!"**

The Priest then turns and walks to the altar where he stands on the east side facing west holding his athame with its point up before him.[8]

---

[8] The athame held by the Priest with its point up is the symbol of the phallic power of the God, which is in this case offered to the Goddess as she is about to be invoked.

As the Priest takes his position by the altar, the Priestess goes to the west where she stands facing out of the Circle. She does an invoking hexagram and says:

"O Ancient One, O Lady of the Moon, we invoke and call upon thee. O triple Goddess, be one with us and within us here in Thy sacred place. May the magick that we do be aided by Thy powers—the powers of Love that were, that are, and that shall ever be. So mote it be!

Everyone says: **"So mote it be!**

The second method for invoking the God and the Goddess is used by the First Temple of the Craft of W.I.C.A. primarily for celebrating the Full Moon, yet, as with any way of working, can be used for any ritual. In this method, the Priestess invokes the God into the Priest and through him into the Circle. The Priest invokes the Goddess into the Priestess and through her into the Circle.

For this version, after completing the elemental invocations the Priest goes to the east where he stands facing into the Circle with his arms outstretched. The Priestess goes to the east and stands before the Priest facing him saying:

"Hear me, O Ancient One, O Lord of Death and Resurrection! Mighty Cernunnos, Consort of the Lady, descend in Thy force and power unto this, your Priest. Be one with him and within him—with us here in this sacred place—that we may know of Your presence by the power we feel within. The power of Life that was, that is, and that shall ever be. So mote it be!"

When the Priestess finishes, she goes to the west where she stands facing into the Circle with arms outstretched. The Priest follows her to the west where he stands before her with his athame raised and says:

"Hear me, O Ancient One, O Lady of the Moon. Descend in Thy crescent grace (if used for the New Moon)/**Thy fullness**

and radiance (if used for the Full Moon)/**Thy Triple Essence** (if used for Festivals) **unto this, Your Priestess. Be one with her and within her, with us here in this sacred place that we may know of Your presence by the Promise** (for a New Moon)/**the Power** (for Full Moon and Festivals) **we feel within. The Promise** (for a New Moon)/**The Power** (for a Full Moon and Festivals) **of Love that was, that is, and that shall ever be. So mote it be!"**

Everyone says: **"So mote it be!"**

At the finish of the ritual, once the forces have been thanked and dismissed, the God and the Goddess should also be thanked for Their attendance and assistance and wished a fond farewell. So the Priest, after dismissing the forces, goes to the east and faces out of the Circle. He does a dismissing hexagram followed by a farewell salutation to the God. Once the Priest has finished, the Priestess goes to the west where facing out she does a dismissing hexagram and a farewell salutation to the Goddess. Neither farewell salutation is scripted at the First Temple of the Craft of W.I.C.A. Each ritual raises different energies and feelings that give rise to the words that should flow from the heart when saying thank you and farewell to the God and the Goddess.

Those are the ritual elements common to almost every ritual done by the First Temple of the Craft of W.I.C.A. Rather than repeat each of these common ritual elements and their instructions over and over again for the rituals that follow in this book, they will be referred to in the ritual text as "cast Circle" or "dismiss Forces." To keep from having to flip back and forth between this chapter and whatever ritual you are working, you might want to copy down each of these common ritual elements on separate sheets of paper or on index cards. Then, as you need them, they will be readily available. In time, as you do more and more ritual work they will become a part of you that you do by and from the heart.

PART II

CELEBRATING
FAMILY TIMES OF CHANGE

Two join as one, their lives to share.
> Hopes, fears, and joys, to each other
> they bear.

A family is formed, their lives rearranged,
> This celebration of family is a Time of
> Change.

In time their love brings birth.
> A child appears carrying joy and mirth.

Expanded now, family life is rearranged.
> This celebration of family is a Time of
> Change.

From birth to death, the cycle moves along.
> Souls continuing ever, in a never-ending
> song.

What lives must die, lives are rearranged.
> This celebration of Death is a Time of
> Change.

CHAPTER 3

A TIME OF JOINING— THE HANDFASTING

TWO PEOPLE meet and feel that their paths run so close that they feel as one. They know one another in mind and heart, in body and soul. They are one! They go forth and seek a formal bonding to become husband and wife, lord and lady, pledged to one another in life. In most of society, the sealing of their bond would be called a marriage ceremony.

In the Wiccan religion such a union is called a *Handfasting*, to "make fast" the hands of one person to those of another. In days of old, to make fast meant to bind something together in a way that was so tight and so close that nothing could work its way in between to separate that which had been so joined.

In most (but not all) Wiccan traditions, handfastings are done in one of two ways following an old custom, though with slightly different meanings. Like many traditions, the First Temple of the Craft of W.I.C.A. performs, according to the wishes of the couple, one of two different types of handfastings, each of which confers different responsibilities upon the two people joined.

The first type of handfasting ritual is one that binds the couple for a year and a day, a trial "marriage" wherein the couple can get to know each other more completely. The idea is that after living together for a year and a day, there should be little doubt as to whether there is a bond of real love joining the two people or if they are together simply because of a physical infatuation. Actually, our society, in general, would probably see a decrease in the divorce rate if the Wiccan year and a day concept was accepted as a common practice.

The year and a day handfasting comes from an old custom, though the meaning behind its use has changed completely. In days long past, the bond joining a couple could be, and in many cases was, provisioned on the woman's ability to bear children. If the woman was unable to conceive within a year and a day, the marriage could be, and usually was, dissolved. Our ancestors, unfortunately, did not realize that the cause for infertility might be with the man and not the woman.

Today, the use of the year and a day handfasting is based on the uncertainty of the individuals' ability to maintain the relationship rather than on their ability to bear children. In fact, the year and a day handfasting today is provisioned upon the couple living together, but refraining from conceiving children during this period. Lovemaking is encouraged as long as the couple takes reasonable precautions to prevent conception. In a year and a day handfasting, contraception is just as much the man's responsibility as it is the woman's responsibility. It is a shared responsibility! When one or both of the people involved in a year and a day handfasting are fully aware of the responsibilities—both emotional and financial—and the work involved with being a single parent, and are able to accept these responsibilities, they may conceive during the year and a day trial period. This is not to say that they expect to separate and become single parents, but rather that they acknowledge the possibility and the resulting responsibilities.

During the year and a day handfasting, the couple shares the path before them with the intention of developing the foundation for a lasting, permanent relationship. This type of handfasting can be dissolved by the Priest and Priestess who performed the ceremony at any time the couple asks to separate. However, the Priest and Priestess will usually encourage and counsel the couple if the union appears to be faltering within the first month or two, when the couple begins to face the realities of living together and the initial infatuation tones down. Encouragement and support at this time can help greatly. In those instances when the couple has given their union time and energy, yet feel that after all their effort their paths are not as close as they had believed, the couple may have the bond dissolved in a formal ceremony; or they may simply wait out the year and a day and then go their separate ways.

For the couples whose paths are truly intertwined, after a year and a day they go through a formal ceremony to reaffirm their vows. This time, the ceremony is one to forge the bonds for life. While the initial year and a day ceremony might have been one of simplicity with a few guests, the second ceremony will usually have all the trappings of a formal wedding. The year and a day follow up ceremony will be similar to the "forever" ceremony that we go through next. The follow up ceremony would begin with an opening like

"We meet here this day to bring together for the second time this couple [Names], who a year and a day ago stood before us and pledged their vows to be as one for the period which has just ended. They are now before us to reaffirm their commitment to each other, but this time, not for a mere year and a day, but forever."

As with any handfasting ceremony, the service should be personalized according to the couple's desires. Having gone through the year and a day ceremony already, the couple will have a good ritual background to build on.

The second type of handfasting is one that is performed when for whatever reason—be it karmic bond or karmic debt—the individuals *know* that they should be together and with serious reflection decide to waive the year and a day trial period. The bonding of this handfasting is serious and the commitment needs to be firm, not based on a whim or infatuation. This handfasting marks the blending of two souls whose paths, while distinct and individual, from this point forward will begin to merge until they become so close as be indistinguishable. Included in this type of handfasting are the pomp and ceremony, the frills and festivities that make a wedding a once in a lifetime event.

In the two handfasting rituals that follow only the vows differentiate the year and a day handfasting from the forever and a day handfasting. The intentions of the individuals expressed in the vows—not the actual ritual—demonstrate which type of handfasting is being celebrated.

The rituals that follow are complete and meant for use either as is, or, for those with ritual experience, adapted as needed to fit the particular backgrounds of the couple involved. The Temple/Altar setups are those that are used by the First Temple of the Craft of W.I.C.A. Though a good guideline, these setups should be changed and adapted to fit the specific wishes of the couple being handfasted. It is their day!

As Wicca is a nature religion, it is excellent to use an outdoor setting such as a park or a forest preserve for the ceremony. Remember, in these cases, a permit for the use of the park or forest reserve area will usually be required and the space, because of demand, will have to be reserved early. By obtaining a permit for a specific area, in most instances, you will have the right to keep uninvited "guests" away. Since most couples will want to oversee or actually help with the setup on site, and it is normally not a good idea for them to come dressed for the ritual, a changing area will be necessary. When using an outdoor setting, therefore, it is a good idea to check the restroom areas in advance to see if they can be used by the bride and groom for changing. If they cannot be used, then it would be wise to arrange for a closed van or a small tent to be put up on site as a changing area.

In decorating an outdoor setting, the desires of the couple should be taken into consideration. Some people would be very upset to see many flowers—once living, now a sacrifice—decorating an already green space. Though, there are others who feel that in this time of celebration some sacrifice is necessary—an offering, so to speak, for the happiness of the couple. For the most part, Mother Nature usually does quite nicely in Her natural decorating of the site.

Now read the rituals that follow. Feel them. Enjoy them. Use them, but most of all—share them!

Handfasting Ritual—Version One
For a Year and a Day

This ritual was originally done outdoors at the 6th Annual Pan Pagan Festival in 1982 and was not a year and a day version, but has been amended here to show such a version.

The area was a large meadow with a pond running along two sides. The altar was set in the center of what would be the Circle, and it was set up in the usual manner. (See chapter 2 for a description of basic altar set up.) In addition, the altar was decorated with flowers, as was the perimeter of the Circle itself. Beside the altar to the north is the broom the couple will jump over later during the ceremony.

The rings of the Lord and Lady being handfasted lie on a pentagram on the altar. Across the pentagram is draped a sash of pure white linen which will be used for the binding. The athame of the Lord being handfasted and the chalice of the Lady being handfasted are also on the altar.

All are gathered to form a Circle except the Lord being handfasted, who stands just beyond the Circle in the east, and the Lady being handfasted, who stands just beyond the Circle in the west. Those people attending who are in Wicca form an inner circle. Friends and relatives who are not in Wicca form a second outer circle. Both groups leave openings in the east and in the west for the Lord and Lady to enter the Circle. Just enough space is left between the two circles for the Priestess to walk through to formally cast the Circle. Near the altar two maidens stand to act for the Priestess as summoners.

The Circle is cast allowing a gateway in the east for the Lord to enter through and a gateway in the west for the Lady to enter through. The gateways may be "framed" by the parents of the Lord in the East and the parents of the Lady in the West, if so desired.

The Mighty Forces, the God, and the Goddess are invoked.

PRIEST: May the place of this rite be consecrated before the Gods, for we gather here in a ritual of Love for Two who would be handfasted!

PRIESTESS: May [_name of the Lord_] and [_name of the Lady_] be brought forward to stand here before us and before the Gods of Nature.

All chant, **"Evo, Evo, Evohe, Salute Diana"** and the Priestess sends the maidens forth to bring the Lord and the Lady into the inner Circle. One maiden attending each, the Lord and Lady stand about three feet inside the Circle facing each other.

PRIESTESS: Be one with us here, O Beings of Air! Intertwine completely the thoughts of Love these two have for one another, that in mind for a year and a day—and longer if they so choose—they shall be as one!

PRIEST: Be one with us here, O Beings of Fire! Kindle their love until it flames with an all-consuming passion burning continuously throughout this year and a day!

PRIESTESS: Be one with us here, O Beings of Water! Fill their Spirits' deep wells of feeling that even when apart they will sense each other's Soul—and touch!

PRIEST: Be one with us here, O Beings of Earth! Steadfast and firm shall you form this bond, that for this year and a day these two shall desire to remain together, that no force from without or within during this time shall prevail against it.

PRIESTESS: Blessed Goddess and Smiling God give to these before us Your Love and Your Protection! Blessed Be!

ALL: Blessed Be!

The Priestess goes to the Lady and the Priest goes to the Lord. They take them by the hand and lead them to stand facing each other before the altar.

PRIEST: Do you [_name of the Lord_] and you [_name of the Lady_] truly meet in Perfect Love and Perfect Trust?

LORD AND LADY: We do!

PRIEST: Then show your Love and Trust for one another at this time.

The Lord and Lady together open their auras to each other, embrace, and kiss.

PRIEST: So Mote It Be!

PRIESTESS: So Mote It Be!

ALL: So Mote It Be!

The Priest hands the Lord the ring of his Lady. The Lord takes the ring and consecrates it. The Priestess hands the Lady the ring of her Lord. The Lady takes the ring and consecrates it. The Lord and Lady then go to the East side of the altar and stand facing each other. The Priest takes the white sash from the altar and binds their left hands together while the Priestess says the following:

PRIESTESS: Above you are the stars in the heavens. Below you is the solid ground. As the seasons pass on remember. . .

Like the Stars your love should be ever bright with the twinkle of happiness!

Like the Heavens your love should be vast beyond seeing!

Like the solid ground your love should be firm and enduring throughout this time.

Possess one another—yet be understanding of the meaning of freedom.

Have patience with one another, for troubles and storms will come—but they will pass quicker in the shelter of each other's arms—and love.

Be free in giving of affection and warmth. A gentle word and a soft touch cost little, but are some of the most priceless treasures of love.

Make love often and be sensuous to one another. Seek to give pleasure and show the awareness of pleasure received.

Fear not the ways and the words of those who do not understand the ways of Wicca, for the Goddess and the God are with you now and always!

The Lady now says the vows she has written while she places the ring on the finger of her Lord. The Lord, then, follows saying the vows he has written, while he places the ring on the finger of his Lady. When they are done, the Priestess unties the white binding sash while the Priest says the following:

PRIEST: With a handfasting, love begins to change the daily words of life into songs and hymns of praise with music that is composed by night to be sung in the light of day. Here and now love's longing draws back the veil and illuminates the recesses of the heart, creating a joy and happiness that none can surpass until the final union with the Great Unmanifest.

A handfasting is the joining of two divinities for a space of time within the cosmos. It is the union of two souls in a strong love seeking complete togetherness. It is that higher unity which will fuse the separate entities within the two spirits.

A handfasting is a golden ring in a chain whose beginning is a first glance, and whose ending may be eternity. It is a pure rain falling from an unblemished sky to fructify and bless the fields of Divine Nature.

As the first glance from the eyes of the beloved is like a seed sown in the human heart, and the first kiss like a flower blooming upon a branch of the Tree of Life, so, now, this union of two lovers becomes the first fruit of that first flower of that seed.

By the Gods, thou art pronounced Lord and Lady of the same holding from this day until the Wheel of Life has turned one full cycle and has passed this day once more.

The Lord and the Lady now perform the symbolic Great Rite.

LADY [Taking her chalice of wine from the altar and holding it before her]: **Before the Goddess and the God have I pledged myself for a year and a day to thee, and to thee alone. So, now, do I offer my maidenhood to thee in the form of this chalice.**

LORD: [Taking his athame from the altar and holding it with both hands directly over the chalice]: **Before the God and the Goddess have I pledged myself for a year and a day to thee, and to thee alone. So, now, do I offer my manhood to thee in the form of this athame.** [The Lord plunges the athame into the chalice and holds it there for a minute, symbolizing a ritual consummation of the marriage. He then places his athame on the altar and the Lord and the Lady share the chalice.]

When they have finished, the Priestess takes the broom[1] and places it on the ground before the couple. Hand in hand, the Lord and Lady jump over the broom. The Priestess picks up the broom and sweeps the past and any old evils from behind the couple to the north and out of the Circle.

The Priest and Priestess each trace an earth-invoking "good wishes" pentagram into the aura of the joined couple after which the couple close their auras.

Beginning in the East, the couple now goes clockwise around the Circle, dismissing each of the Mighty Forces at each of the four quarters.

LORD AND LADY: Mighty Forces of the [_name quarter_] we thank thee for attending our handfasting, but if go ye must, we say hail, [kiss wrist] and farewell. [Repeat for each quarter until all four are dismissed.]

The Priest dismisses the God. The Priestess dismisses the Goddess and then uncasts the Circle.

---

[1] The broom used in a handfasting can be either a broom that belongs to the Coven and is "traditionally" used for handfastings or, for a nice touch, it can be a special broom made or purchased for the couple being handfasted.

ALL: So Mote It Be!

In the handfasting ritual just presented, there are several areas that may require some explanation for a beginner in Wicca. Overall, the ritual follows the same basic format of all our rituals. The handfasting starts with a Circle casting and the invocation of the Mighty Forces and the God and Goddess. It proceeds, similar to a festival, through the working to the conclusion where the Mighty Forces, the God, and the Goddess are thanked and dismissed. The ritual ends with the Circle being uncast. As you begin to adapt your own version of a handfasting, within the ritual are several items that you should make part of any handfasting ritual.

First, as any wedding, the Lord and the Lady—call them the Bride and the Groom if you wish—are the reason for the ritual taking place at all. Therefore, the ritual is not started with the Lord and Lady simply as parts of the Circle, but with each of them making an entrance so that everyone present can focus their energies on these two who will shortly be a couple. This is not merely pomp and ceremony. Rather, it is a serious part of centering the energy for this most magickal event.

In most rituals, once the Circle has been cast, the auras of those present are opened to the energies that will be raised as part of the particular ritual. In a handfasting, the energies that are being raised in the circle are specifically for the couple being handfasted. So, here, the only auras that are opened to the energies of the Circle and of each other are the auras of the couple being handfasted.

Next, though the Mighty Forces have been invoked at the beginning after the Circle is cast, they are petitioned again. They are invoked this time specifically to bring aspects of each of the elements into the relationship being formed by the couple. Both the God and the Goddess are petitioned again on behalf of the couple.

In turn, the binding of the couple's left hands with the white sash or cord is significant, of course, making fast their hands—one to one another—the Handfasting. The sash or cord used is white, signifying the harmonious blending of all the colors of the rainbow with all of their energies as well—a positive binding with all energies, so that the couple will start off firmly, lacking in none.

Within the handfasting ceremony, things, like the vows, which are personal, can and should be done by the couple themselves. Embellishments to the ceremony can be added as the couple or the coven chooses. We had a handfasting that borrowed one element from the science fiction movie *Krull*. As long as it worked, there was no problem with it.

Following the vows and the removal of the now unneeded symbol, the sash, is the couple's performance of the symbolic Great Rite—the symbolic act of the consummation of the marriage.[2] The chalice is the symbol of the Lady's maidenhood now offered unprotected in love and trust to her Lord. It is his to fulfill. Likewise, the athame is the symbol of the Lord's manhood and power now offered in love and trust to his Lady. It is hers to fulfill. It is this equal giving, each to the other, symbolized in this act that culminates the magick of this ritual.

After the Great Rite, they are one, and hand in hand, jump over the broom, leaving their individual pasts behind as they start together on the new path before them. Along with the past, they leave behind any negativity—including apprehensions regarding this handfasting—which may have come with them to this point. These unwanted energies are swept (grounded) out of the Circle by the Priestess.

Finally, as the Mighty Forces were petitioned in the beginning of the ritual to give special blessings to the couple, it is fitting that the Lord and Lady give thanks to each of the Mighty Forces as they do the dismissals.

---

[2] In some groups, in some instances when a permanent handfasting is being performed, rather than a symbolic Great Rite, the couple will actually consummate the marriage in a side room or a tent before the festivities continue.

Figure 2. The Handfasting Altar. Decorated with fresh flowers with the couple's rings on the center pentacle, and just beyond, the white cord for the binding.

Figure 3. The couple standing before the altar. Note the broom lying on the ground beside the altar.

Figure 4. Left: The couple with their hands bound fast with the white cord. Right: The couple reciting their vows over the cup.

Figure 5. Left: The Lady adding herbs to the cup as part of the sharing. Right: Sharing from the cup.

Figure 6. Jumping the broom.

Figure 7. A strong embrace while the Priestess sweeps away the past with the broom.

Figure 8. A shared toast.

Figure 9. A traditional first sharing of cake.

Handfasting Ritual—Version Two
For Now and For Always

My own handfasting was a double handfasting that did not include the traditional symbolic Great Rite because the other couple was uncomfortable with it. In the following description of my handfasting, I have inserted a footnote reference at the moment during the ritual when it would have been done. The exchange that Dorothy and I shared over the chalice to formalize our union in lieu of the symbolic Great Rite is also included. I have revised my handfasting here to a single, rather than a double handfasting.

The altar is arranged in the usual manner. In addition, it is bedecked with flowers, as is the perimeter of the Circle. On the pentacle on the altar lie the rings of the Lord and Lady. Draped across the pentacle is a white sash for the binding. To the west of the pentacle is a large chalice. To the north of the pentacle is a small dish of herbs.[3] (See figure 2 on page 46.)

The bell is rung to gather the people to form the Circle. For this handfasting there is only one circle. Friends and relatives who are not of the Wiccan religion stand side by side with those who practice Wicca to form a single circle of love and trust. Gateways are left in the East and in the West for Lord Stanley and Lady Dorothy to enter through. At the Circle's edge in the south are several musicians with guitars.

Lord Stanley stands just beyond the Circle in the East with his attendant. Lady Dorothy stands just beyond the Circle in the West with her attendant.

---

[3] As part of our handfasting, during our vows we each added a blend of herbs to the chalice we would share. The herbs were selected for what they would bring into the union through their mystical properties. As I was bringing in what would be considered the masculine or God aspects, my herbs were: Chamomile, for money; Comfrey, for protection; and Angelica, for a long life together. My Lady was bringing the feminine or Goddess aspects into the union, and the herbs she added were: Myrtle, for blessings and good luck; Peppermint, for harmony; and Vervain, for dreams and wishes to come true. For love, we both added Damiana.

The Circle for this ritual is cast by having everyone join hands one by one beginning in the East and following clockwise around, leaving a space in the west and a space in the east. They are asked to channel love to their neighbor as they join hands so that the Circle might be cast as a ring of love that will surround the couple.

Once the Circle has been cast, the Mighty Forces, the God, and the Goddess are invoked.

PRIEST: May the place of this rite be consecrated before the Gods, for we gather here in a ceremony of love for two who would become one!

PRIESTESS: May Lady Dorothy and Lord Stanley be brought forth to stand before us and before the Gods of Nature.

The musicians begin to play as the attendants bring the couple into the Circle to stand together, side by side, facing the altar in the east. (See figure 3 on page 46.)

PRIESTESS: Be one with this couple here, O Beings of Air! Intertwine completely the thoughts of love that they have for each other. Grant that in mind, henceforth, that they shall complement one another and be as one!

PRIEST: Be one with this couple here, O Beings of Fire! Kindle the feelings of love that they have for each other until they flame with an all-consuming passion that will burn endlessly throughout the Aeons!

PRIESTESS: Be one with this couple here, O Beings of Water! Fill their spirits' deep wells of feeling until they overflow and run together so that even when they are apart they will sense each other's soul and touch!

PRIEST: Be one with this couple here, O Beings of Earth! Steadfast and firm shall ye form this bond upon which

they build so that so long as this couple desires to be together, no force from within or without shall prevail against their love!

PRIESTESS: Blessed Goddess and Shining God—give to this couple before us Your love and Your protection! Blessed Be!

ALL: Blessed Be!

PRIEST: Do you, Lady Dorothy, and you, Lord Stanley, truly meet in perfect love and perfect trust?

LADY DOROTHY & LORD STANLEY [together]: We do!

PRIESTESS: Then show your love and trust for each other at this time.

Lady Dorothy and Lord Stanley open their auras, embrace, and kiss.

PRIEST: So Mote It Be!

ALL: So Mote It Be!

The Priest takes the sash from across the pentacle then lifts the pentacle with the rings and holds it before Lady Dorothy, who picks up the ring for her Lord. She consecrates the ring with the four elements, channeling her personal energy into it as well. When she is finished, Lord Stanley picks up the ring for his Lady. He consecrates the ring with the four elements, channeling his energy into it as well.

The Priest places the pentacle back on the altar and picks up the sash. He asks the Lord and the Lady to face each other and extend their left hands. The Priest binds their left hands with the white sash. (See figure 4 on page 47.) As the Priest does the binding, the Priestess says:

Above you are the stars in the heavens. Beneath you rests the solid ground. As time passes, remember:

Like the stars, your love for each other should be ever bright with the twinkle of happiness ever sparkling in your eyes.

Like the heavens, your love for each other should be vast unto infinity.

Like the solid ground, your love for each other should be firm and enduring throughout the ages as shown by your embraces given daily.

Possess one another, but be ever understanding of the meaning of freedom.

Have patience with each other, for storms and problems will come, but they will pass ever so quickly if you stand in the shelter of each other's arms with love.

Be free in the giving of attention and warmth. A gentle word and a soft touch cost little, yet they are some of the most priceless treasures of love.

Make love often and be sensuous with one another. Fear not to give pleasure, nor to show the awareness of pleasure received.

Fear not the ways and words of others around you. In your love for each other the God and the Goddess are with you—now and forever!

Lady Dorothy places the ring on Lord Stanley's finger and gives her vows. Lord Stanley places the ring on Lady Dorothy's finger and gives his vows.

The Priestess picks up the chalice and hands it to the couple who hold it in their left hands [still bound]. The Priest picks up the dish of herbs and holds it before the couple. (See figure 5 on page 47.)

LADY DOROTHY: Into this union I come to share with you the blessings of the God and the Goddess. [She takes a pinch of the herbs and drops it into the chalice of wine.]

LORD STANLEY: Into this union I come to share with you protection and comfort. [He takes a pinch of herbs and drops it into the chalice of wine.]

LADY DOROTHY: Into this union I come to share with you harmony. [She takes a pinch of herbs and drops it into the chalice of wine.]

LORD STANLEY: Into this union I come to share with you prosperity. [He takes a pinch of herbs and drops it into the chalice of wine.]

LADY DOROTHY: Into this union I come to share with you dreams together. [She takes a pinch of herbs and drops it into the chalice of wine. See figure 5 on page 47.]

LORD STANLEY: Into this union I come to share with you health and long life together. [He takes a pinch of herbs and drops it into the chalice of wine.]

LADY DOROTHY [Takes the chalice from the Priestess]: **To seal this union of love, I offer you this Cup of Cerridwen— this Holy Grail of Love's Immortality—to share with me, to signify the life we shall share together.**

LORD STANLEY [Takes the cup and drinks deeply]: **And back to thee do I offer to share this Cup of Cerridwen—and my life—forever.** [See figure 5 on page 47.]

He offers the cup to Lady Dorothy who drinks deeply from it and[4] then hands it back to the Priestess who places it back on the altar. The Priestess unties the white binding sash as the Priest says:

---

[4] The symbolic Great Rite in this ritual would be done at this time. Instead of handing the chalice back to the Priestess, the Lady would hold it before her and say, **"By this chalice before the Goddess and the God do I pledge my maidenhood to thee and to thee alone!"** The Lord, taking his athame, would hold it above the chalice and say, **"By this athame before the God and the Goddess do I pledge my manhood to thee and to thee alone!"** The Lord would then plunge his athame into the chalice and hold it there as together they say, **"One with one another—forever!"** Then the Lady would hand the chalice back to the Priestess.

With a handfasting, love begins to change the daily words of life into songs of praise with music that is composed by night to be sung in the light of day.

Here, now, love's longing draws back the veil and illumines the recesses of the heart, creating a joy and happiness that no one can surpass.

A handfasting is the joining of two Divine Spirits so that a third might be brought forth upon the Earth.

It is the total union of two souls striving for completeness.

A handfasting fosters that higher unity in which the individuals within these two spirits will be fused.

It is the Golden Ring in a chain whose beginning is that first glance and whose ending is eternity itself.

It is the pure, fresh rain falling from a cloudless sky to fructify and bless the fields of Divine Nature.

That first glance from the eyes of the beloved is as a seed sown in the heart. Their first kiss is as a flower upon a branch of the Tree of Life. This union of two lovers, now, is as the first fruit of that first flower of that seed!

By the Gods thou art pronounced Lord and Lady unto one another!

The Priestess places the broom, on the ground before the couple. Hand in hand the couple jumps the broom (See figure 6 on page 48.) The Priestess then takes the broom and sweeps the past away and out of the Circle in the north. (See figure 7 on page 48.)

The Priest and Priestess now present the couple to each of the quarters, and the couple give their thanks at each. The Mighty Forces are *not* dismissed, as they are welcome to join in the festivities. They will be dismissed later by the Priest and Priestess as the festivities are winding down.

PRIEST & PRIESTESS [Together before each of the quarters in turn]: **Mighty Forces of the *[particular quarter]*we bring to you Lord Stanley and Lady Dorothy joined this day in a union of love!**

LORD STANLEY & LADY DOROTHY [Together before each of the quarters in turn]: **Mighty Forces of the [*particular quarter*] we thank you for attending our handfasting and for the energies shared. Blessed Be!**

ALL: Blessed Be!

The couple closes their auras.

PRIESTESS: We are going to open the Circle of love we made earlier when we all joined hands. So, if everyone would please turn around and face the outside of the Circle and push the Circle of love we formed out and away from where you stand. See it growing larger as it moves farther and farther away. Like a ripple on a large pond, see it moving out and away . . . to the edge of the park . . . to the edge of the city . . . to the edge of the state . . . rippling out and away until it meets itself. So that we may truly say, The Circle is open, yet Unbroken! So Mote It Be!

ALL: So Mote It Be!

As the musicians begin to play, the Priest and Priestess ask everyone to fall in behind the couple to march over to where the refreshments are for a toast to the new couple. (See figures 8 and 9 on page 49.)

These handfasting ceremonies are given as examples to show the various elements that the First Temple of the Craft of W.I.C.A. has put together to form the handfasting ceremonies that we perform. I am sure there are elements that some other groups use in their handfasting ceremonies that we do not use simply because we are not aware of them. My purpose is to open up to others one way so that all may know and grow from it. I hope that others will share their rituals too, so that we all can grow. Blessed Be!

CHAPTER 4

YOUNG AWAKENING—
THE WICCANING

THE HANDFASTING acknowledges the family core—the husband and wife. In time, most couples will have children and the family will grow in size and responsibilities. As children grow, Wiccan parents—especially those who were brought up in any of the various Christian sects—start to have questions regarding their children's participation in the Wiccan religion. Most of these parents remember the Christian ceremony of baptism and its dual concept of both bringing the child into the particular faith as well as placing the child under the protection/salvation of that faith's God. Questions often asked by parents are: Does the Wiccan religion have a ceremony similar to baptism? Should we train our children in the Wiccan religion? And, if we should, at what age should we begin to bring them into the Circle?

To start with the last question first, at the First Temple of the Craft of W.I.C.A. we believe that a child's questions regarding our faith should be answered truthfully, but with only as much information as the child can understand at his or her age level. If you, the child, and the coven are all comfortable with children being in Circle then you should have your children go and stand beside you in Circle, just as parents in Christian sects take their children to church. It is recommended that children start by attending festivals first and then New Moon celebrations. Because of the high energy levels at Full Moon celebrations, it is not recommended for children to attend until they are old enough to fully comprehend what the ritual entails.

As for training our children in the ways of Wicca, I believe children should be exposed to our ways and have their questions about Wicca answered. So that when they reach an age at which they are making decisions for themselves, they can consciously choose whether to make it their path or not.

Just as Christian sects have baptism rituals, the Wiccan religion has a Wiccaning for the child. However, while a baptism not only places the child under the protection of the faith's God but also bonds the child—in some cases forever—to that particular faith, a Wiccaning only introduces the child to the Mighty Forces, the God, and Goddess and asks for their aid and protection for the child. There is no intention of any lifetime bonding to the religion itself. In a Wiccaning the parents bring forth the child and present him or her to the Priest and Priestess asking for blessings upon the child. The Priest and Priestess call upon the God and the Goddess to bless and give special gifts to the child. Then, the Priest and Priestess present the child to each of the quarters and ask for protection for the child. As part of the Wiccaning ceremony a formal calling forth and introduction of the couple or persons chosen by the parents as the child's godparents may also be done. This publicly expresses the will of the parents as to who shall be vested with the child's care and safety should the parents be called over the veil early in the child's life.

A Wiccaning is not a dedication of the child to the Wiccan religion. That is a decision that children should be allowed to make on their own when they are older. Just as the Wiccan religion does not try to convert others to the faith by cornering them on street corners, neither does it try to convert small unknowing children. If the Wiccan faith is to truly be theirs, it must be entered into with full awareness and consent.

Because the Wiccaning can be filled with so much meaning, like the handfasting it should **not** exclude anyone simply because he or she is not of the Wiccan religion. It is a family time of change and therefore, the Circle should be of the family. Family, here includes those who are related by blood, those who are of the Wiccan religion, as well as those who are friends and part of the child's daily routine "family." Because some of those who attend the Wiccaning are not of the Wiccan religion and may not know the meaning of the event, it is always a good idea for one of the parents or the Priest or Priestess to begin the Wiccaning with a short explanation of the ritual. Such an introduction brings everyone together so that they may appreciate their participation more and raise more energy for the child. It also educates those who are not Wiccan about who we are and what we do.

While baptisms are done as soon as possible in Christian sects for fear that an unbaptized child would somehow be left out of their God's plan of things, the Wiccaning can be done whenever the parents feel that the time is right for the child. Some Wiccanings have been done for children as old as 10. Most of the time, however, the Wiccaning will be done by the time the child is 5. As a child's formative years run from birth through age 3 and 4, doing a Wiccaning on a child's first or second birthday can leave a solid impression. By coupling the Wiccaning with the child's birthday you also reinforce the event and can make it one terrific birthday party!

In preparation for the Wiccaning, there are several things that the parents need to do.

First, they should inform their Priest and Priestess that they would like to set a date for a Wiccaning for their child. It is a good idea to give your Priest and Priestess at least six months advance notification if possible. At the same time, it is a good idea to get the reservations for the site of the Wiccaning if it is to be in a park or county recreational area. Just as we encourage people to do the Handfasting ceremony outside, so, too, we believe the Wiccaning ceremony can be most beautiful when done together in Nature's beauty. If possible, the site should be one that is special to the couple.

Next, if the announcement of the child's godparents is to be a part of the Wiccaning, the couple should choose who the godparents will be and discuss it with them to make sure that the prospective godparents are comfortable with the responsibility of the position.

Invitations need to be sent to those expected to attend. We recommend asking for an R.S.V.P. if the site has size limitations or if refreshments will be served. As this gathering is an open one and will usually include people of other religions, it is a good idea to include on the invitations to those who are Wiccan whether robes are optional or not.

Figure 10. The Priest and Priestess with the child to be Wiccaned.

Figure 11. Left: Presentation of the gift (stone) by the Guardian of the West. Right: Presentation of the gift (stone) by the Guardian of the North.

Figure 12. Left: Priestess giving the gift (silver) of the Goddess. Right: Priest giving the gift (gold) of the God.

Figure 13. Left: Sharing the cup with the new Godparents. Right: Sharing the cup with the newly Wiccaned child.

Figure 14. Left: "It's ALL mine!" Right: A happy time!

The child needs a white robe, cape, or ritual garment for the Wiccaning. If it can be made by the child's parents, it will carry that extra love into the Circle for the child.

Finally, the couple should go over the ritual with the Priest and Priestess. There may be some special people who are close to the family and would like to be part of the ritual. A Wiccaning is not a time for coven formality. The ritual should be open to anyone who will bring love into the Circle and benefit the child.

What follows is a Wiccaning as done by the First Temple of the Craft of W.I.C.A. As with any of the rituals in this book, it may be used verbatim or it may be amended to suit those involved. It is one way that we do Wiccanings—it is not the only way to do Wiccanings.

Wiccaning Ritual

The site is an outdoor park area large enough for thirty to forty people to form a circle around a center altar. The site is only decorated with what nature has provided. Nothing is added to the natural beauty of summer.

The altar is covered with a white altar cloth and set up in the usual manner. In addition, on the altar is a chalice of apple juice, a small cake, and a small pouch that has been made to hold the gifts that will be given to the child by each of the elements, the God, and the Goddess.

Prior to the ritual starting, each of the people representing a quarter element will have received the gemstone he or she will be giving to the child in the ritual as a "gift". The gold and silver "gifts" of the God and the Goddess can either be carried by the Priest and the Priestess or be to one side of the altar.

The bell is rung and the people are gathered and asked to form a Circle around the altar. The parents whose child is being Wiccaned stand with their child in the north. Because in the First Temple of the Craft of W.I.C.A. we seek a balanced polarity if there is a cluster of men or women at a point of the

Circle, the Priest or Priestess will break up the cluster and balance the Circle male/female/male/female as best they can.

The Priest or the Priestess turns to the Circle and gives a brief explanation of a Wiccaning and of the ritual about to be done. As each coven has its own traditions, the specifics of each ritual may differ; so it is good to brief those attending from other groups on the specifics so that they do not expect something that will not happen. When the explanation is over, the Circle is cast and the Priest begins.

PRIEST: We start this Wiccaning by joining hands—one with one another—in love. And as we take the hand of the person next to us, be they a close companion or a new acquaintance, there is a bond formed—a bond of fellowship and love—which is shared at that moment and then which flows around this Circle joining all present together. At the same time as this flow of love goes around the Circle, it also radiates forward to fill the center of this Circle with our feelings of love and protection, of care and hope and joy for [_name of child being Wiccaned_]. Feel and be aware of that love that we share here today!

PRIESTESS: Beyond our beings exist the higher forces of life called by some the Guardians, by others the Archangelics, by still others the Kings of the Elements. At this time do we recognize their presence here.

EAST [Stepping forward from his or her place in the east]: **East—the element of Air! We feel and know the air all around us. . .In the howling blast of Winter. . .In the awakening winds of Spring. . .In the gentle breezes of Summer. . .In the leaf filled whirlwinds of Fall. The element of Air fills us with inspiration with every breath that we take. Breathe, feel, and know within you the element of Air!**

SOUTH [Stepping forward from his or her place in the South]: **South—the element of Fire! We feel and know the element of Fire in each radiant ray of the sun. Its warmth**

gives hope in Winter. . .Awakens new life in Spring. . .Heats up all growth in Summer. . .And warms all through maturity in Fall. Fire is life! Feel the radiant rays of the sun as they warm you at this time and know within you the element of Fire!

WEST [Stepping forward from his or her place in the West]: West—the element of Water! We feel and know the element of Water with each morning's dew. In the icy snows of Winter. . .In the thunderstorms of Spring. . .In the gentle rains of Summer. . .In the chilling rains of Autumn we feel and know this flowing element that is so much a part of our makeup! Feel and know the Water that is carried always on the wind and rests as well in the earth beneath your feet. Know within you the element of Water!

NORTH [Stepping forward from his or her place in the North]: **North—the element of Earth! We feel and know the element of Earth with each step we take. From the cold frozen surface of Winter. . .To the beginning green of Spring. . .To the brightly colored fields of Summer. . .To the yellowing cover of Fall we feel and know the changes of the earth about us and within us. Feel the earth beneath you at this time and know the strength of its manifestation within you. Know within you the element of Earth!**

The Priest and Priestess stand facing each other at the western edge of the altar and call forth the parents with the child to be Wiccaned.

PRIEST & PRIESTESS: Let [*names of parents*] bring forth their child [*name of child*].

The parents bring their child to the altar and, standing with their backs to the west, hold the child before the Priest and the Priestess.

PRIEST: The Almighty IS! And is beyond our comprehension—and so that we might come to know the Almighty, the

God force without and within, we call upon the Almighty in the Male-God form.

PRIESTESS: Likewise that we may each of us know the balanced polarity of the Almighty, we call upon the Almighty in the Female-Goddess form.

PRIEST & PRIESTESS: Together do we call forth the Almighty into this Circle of Love and into this child [*name of child*]!

They pause for a moment. Then, the Priest raises his hands to the heavens and pulls in the energy, bringing it down with his hands as the Priestess points her hands to the ground, and pulls in the energy from the Earth, bringing it up with her hands to meet with the Priest—hand touching hand—over the child.

PRIEST: That he/she may know of the God and realize His powers of strength—moral, mental, and physical!

PRIESTESS: That he/she may know of the Goddess and realize Her powers of Love—for all things living!

PRIEST: That he/she may know of the God and realize His powers of intellect and reason!

PRIESTESS: That he/she may know of the Goddess and Her powers of intuition and feeling!

PRIEST: That he/she may know of the God and, by so knowing, as he/she matures in years be able to understand the strengths and weaknesses of the men and women he/she will meet in life.

PRIESTESS: That he/she may know of the Goddess and, by so knowing, as he/she matures in years will be able to know and understand the intuitions and feelings of the men and women he/she will meet in life.

PRIEST & PRIESTESS: So Mote It Be!

ALL: So Mote It Be!

PRIEST: But for now [*name of child*] is still a small child much needing of protection. Do you, his/her parents, seek that protection, care, and guidance?

PARENTS: Yes, we do!

PRIESTESS: If this be your wish, then give him/her to us so that we might present him/her to each of the Quarters to receive their gifts. [Priestess picks up pouch from the altar.]

Parents give the child to the Priestess who takes the child to the East where she stands before the Guardian of the East. If handing the child off to the Priestess and Priest could be a problem, the parents can simply walk with the Priestess or Priest to the Quarters. An older child can take the hand of the Priestess or Priest and walk with her or him to each of the Quarters. (See figure 10 on page 60.)

PRIESTESS: You, who are the Guardian of the Powers of the East, I ask you now to give the blessings and protection of that Power to [*name of child*].

EAST: Blessings, Protection—and more will [*name of child*] receive from the Powers of the East! Great source of inspiration, fly to us here on the wings of the wind. Bring to the mind of this child the knowledge that imperative reasoning must receive before action is possible. Mighty Forces of the East, set his/her thoughts firmly upon the path of spiritual renewal. Fill [*name of child*] with a vigorous questioning mind that he/she will always turn from the darkness of ignorance and seek only the illuminating light of truth— and his/her own path toward that light. As a token and

symbol of these gifts do I give to this child this Sacred stone[1] [East places stone in pouch.]

The Priest takes the child and the pouch from the Priestess and goes to the South where he stands before the Guardian of the South.

PRIEST: You, who are the Guardian of the Powers of the South, I ask you now to give the blessings and protection of that Power to [*name of child*].

SOUTH: Blessings, protection—and more will [*name of child*] receive from the Powers of the South! Great Fires of Life, come to us on the beams of the Sun and fill this child with your neverending energy. May his/her life force be ever strong. Mighty Forces of the South, give to this child your energy so that [*name of child*] may go forth in your name and help and heal others and that his/her life force will not falter as he/she moves forward on his/her path! As a token and a symbol of these gifts do I give to this child this sacred stone![2] [South places stone in the pouch.]

The Priestess takes the child and the pouch from the Priest and proceeds to the West where she stands before the Guardian of the West.

PRIESTESS: You who are the Guardian of the Powers of the West, I ask you now to give the blessings and protection of that Power to [*name of child*].

---

[1] If the child's astrological sign is an air sign, the stone should be one from the pair designated for his or her sign in the following list: Gemini—moss agate or chrysoprase; Libra—opal or lapis; Aquarius—garnet or red zircon. Otherwise, use whatever stone feels comfortable from this list.

[2] If the child's astrological sign is a fire sign, use one of the stones designated for that sign in the following list: Aries—diamond or bloodstone; Leo—amber or sardonyx or tourmaline; Sagittarius—chrysolite or golden topaz. Otherwise, use any of these stones.

WEST: Blessings, protection—and more will [_name of child_] receive from the Powers of the West! Great Waters of Emotion, come to us like ocean waves upon the shore and flow around and through this child filling him/her with feeling and intuition. Mighty Forces of the West give to this child awareness of that intuitive power that lies within and connects us all so that [_name of child_] will instinctively know the path that is his/hers to follow. As a token and a symbol of these gifts do I give to this child this sacred stone![3] [West places stone in the pouch. See figure 11 on page 60.]

The Priest takes the child and the pouch from the Priestess and proceeds to the North where he stands before the Guardian of the North.

PRIEST: You who are the Guardian of the Powers of the North, I ask you now to give the blessings and protection of that Power to [_name of child_].

NORTH: Blessings, protection—and more will [_name of child_] receive from the Powers of the North! Strength of the Earth that we feel beneath us, fill this child with your power and stability. Mighty Forces of the North give to [_name of child_] strength of purpose so that he/she may ever walk his/her path with firm resolution undaunted by whatever forces might try to sway [_name of child_] from his/her true journey. As a token and a symbol of these gifts do I give to this child this sacred stone![4] [North places stone in the pouch. See figure 11 on page 60.]

---

[3] If the child's astrological sign is a water sign, use one of the stones designated for that sign in the following list: Pisces—amethyst or peridot; Cancer—moonstone or quartz crystal; Scorpio—aquamarine or beryl. Otherwise, use any of these stones.

[4] If the child's astrological sign is an earth sign, use one of the stones designated for that sign in the following list: Virgo—carnelian or jade; Taurus—turquoise or sapphire; Capricorn—black onyx or jet or malachite. Otherwise, use any of these stones.

The Priest takes the child and the pouch back to the altar where the Priestess and the parents are waiting.

PRIESTESS: As a token and a symbol of the Goddess, who watches over us always, do I give to [_name of child_] this piece of silver. Its silvery sheen mirrors the light of the Lady so that [_name of child_] may always know that the Goddess is with him/her. [Priestess places silver piece in the pouch. See figure 12 on page 61.]

PRIEST: As a token and a symbol of the God, who is ever with us, do I give to [_name of child_] this piece of gold. Its golden radiance shines as does the light of the Sun God overhead so that [_name of child_] may always know that the God is with him/her. [Priest places gold piece in the pouch. See figure 12 on page 61.]

The Priest hands the child and the pouch to the parents.

PARENTS: [_name of child_], the power and the protection of the Almighty now shines over and through you. [Each kisses the child.] **With love in our hearts we will care for you and guide you in the years to come. Yet we, too, realize our mortality and the need that, if we are called away, there will be those who with love would continue to care and guide [_name of child_] down his/her path in life. We would ask that those so chosen step forward and join with us here and now.**

The people that the parents have chosen for godparents come forward to the altar.

PARENTS: With love in your hearts will you pledge to look after and care for [_name of child_] should we be taken away before he/she matures?

GODPARENTS: We do!

PARENTS: With love in your hearts will you pledge to give [_name of child_] guidance and strength should we be

taken away before he/she has sufficient knowledge and strength of his/her own?

GODPARENTS: We will!

The parents hand the child to the godparents.

PARENTS: Then, in token, do we now give [_name of child_] to you and by so doing recognize you as his/her guardians and godparents should anything take us from him/her.

PRIEST: Know all of you present that [_names of the god-parents_] have been so chosen and have accepted these duties and responsibilities this day. Let none contest the wishes of these parents for the welfare of [_name of child_].

PRIESTESS: So Mote It Be!

ALL: So Mote It Be!

The godparents hand the child back to the parents as the Priest picks up the small cake.

PRIEST: We have joined together in a celebration of love for this family. As a family let us now break bread with one another through the sharing of this cake. [Priest holds the cake up to the East.] **Great Lord, join with us and fill this cake with Your strength and energy so that all who share may be strengthened one with one another and know that they may walk their path steadfast in the knowledge that they do not walk alone!**

The Priest shares the cake first with the parents, the child, and the godparents, then with the rest of the Circle. Lastly, he shares with the Priestess.

PRIESTESS [Picking up the chalice from the altar]: **We have joined together in a celebration of love for this family. As**

a family let us now share this cup with one another. [Priestess holds the chalice up to the West.] **Great Lady, join with us and fill this cup with your unbounding love so that all who share may feel the hearts of all the others here with us and know in their own heart that they will always walk their path in love.**

The Priestess shares the cup first with the couple, the child, and the godparents, then with the rest of the Circle. Lastly, she shares the cup with the Priest. (See figures 13 and 14 on page 61.)

PRIESTESS [To the Circle]: **This Circle was formed in love by love. So long as that love remains in your hearts the Circle will stand open—yet unbroken! Blessed Be!**

ALL: Blessed Be!

A Wiccaning is a special moment in time for all concerned. For the parents, it is a time that brings their child the special protections of the God and Goddess as well as the protection of the Elemental Forces. For the child, the Wiccaning marks an infusion of new energies and awareness. For the godparents, this time marks the formal acknowledgment of their new responsibilities. For those attending who are of the Craft, the Wiccaning is a renewing of feelings long ago stored in the unconscious. For those attending who are not of the Craft, it is an opening unto the ways of others that they might come to know us better. All in all, it is a celebration of love that everyone can be a part of and grow from. (See figure 14 on page 61.)

CHAPTER 5

BEYOND THE VEIL—
THE FUNERARY RITE

AS TIME PASSES there are moments in everyone's life when someone who is near and dear ceases existence on this plane and passes beyond the veil. When loved ones pass over, a void is left in the lives of those left behind—a void that if left unfulfilled, will seek to bind the spirit of the departed to this place by its very vacuum. It is necessary—no matter how hard some people may protest against it—to soothe the feelings of loneliness, of heartache, of desperation, in some instances, that may be created by someone's passing. In Wicca, the funerary rite is meant to do these things through the celebration of the evolvement of the person who has passed over.

With a background belief in reincarnation, the Wiccan religion does not fear a hell or some vague eternal damnation for anyone who has passed beyond the veil. Rather, the Wiccan religion embraces a belief that those who have passed over have done so because they have completed all the lessons they were meant to learn in this lifetime and are now enjoying a repose until they are reborn to new lessons in a new life—a process that will continue until they have grown so completely as to pass over and become one with the cosmos ("God").

Because the Wiccan religion views death as a completion of one cycle and an evolvement to the next cycle, like a graduation ceremony it is a time to be happy for the individual who has moved on. Our ways differ from the Christian concepts that give the impression that death, for a "good" person, is an escape from punishment or a reward with a heavenly hereafter. In the Wiccan religion, we view life for what it is—a series of lessons. Some of those lessons may be pleasant while others may be bitter and hard; but they are all a part of living, and as such should be learned and the knowledge derived from those lessons enjoyed. Wicca realizes that life on this Earth is *not* a punishment to be endured, but a joy to be lived. So when the cycle for an individual is complete and the necessary lessons have been learned, the individual passing over is getting a "summer break" from the school of life before classes continue.

Yet for those who have been left behind, there is still a need for consolation for the loss of an intimate companion or good friend. Throughout our lives we encounter changes that require friends to move on and leave us behind—job changes and moves to new homes or better climates are also times when old friends leave. We can brood over the loss or fill that space with new friends. The choice is ours. When someone passes beyond the veil, those who remain have that same choice. They can shut themselves off from growth or open themselves to fill that void with new friendships. A Wiccan funerary rite is usually not complete without a big party to follow the service—a party with food, wine, music, and plenty of friends to gather and share memories of the person who has passed over. In the wee hours of the morning as the party dwindles to a close, all who have attended have let go of their emotional ties to the departed and have opened themselves to the friendships and bonds of the others who also attended. The camaraderie and companionships brought forth allow the strong to be there for the not so strong and allow those with strong emotional ties to the departed to find the strength through their friends to sever those ties and accept this time for what it is—another point on the Wheel of Life.

The funerary service before the party is brief. The service does not need to be a long, drawn out affair, for the service is just the preamble for the celebration that will follow. It is a farewell—not a mourning! It should allow for those close to the departed to express their memories and allow for all to say farewell to their friend. The following poem expresses the idea beautifully.

Do not stand at my grave and weep—
    I am not there, I do not sleep.
For I am a thousand winds that blow,
    I am the diamond glints on the snow
I am the sunlight on the ripened grain,
    I am the gentle autumn rain
When you awaken in the morning hush
    I am the swift uplifting rush
Of gentle birds in circled flight.
    I am the soft stars that light the night.
Do not stand at my grave and cry.
    I am not there. I did not die!

The following is the funerary service currently used by the First Temple of the Craft of W.I.C.A. It is meant to be used at the funeral parlor where the person who has passed beyond the veil has been laid in state. It can, however, be used at a gathering of friends at the home of the deceased or even at the graveside. It will work well at almost any location where family and friends of the departed have come together. For the service the only necessary piece of equipment is a large bell or gong.

The decoration of the site for the service should be discussed with the immediate family and should reflect as best as possible their wishes. Likewise, whether the Priest wears a robe or a suit and the Priestess wears a robe or an appropriate dress should depend on the location of the service and the wishes of the immediate family.

At the scheduled time for the service the Priest and the Priestess should take their places and be introduced by a member of the immediate family of the departed or briefly introduce themselves. Remember, while some of the immediate family and friends may know the Priest and Priestess, there may be people in attendance who have no idea at all as to who they are.

The Priest and the Priestess should start the service by inviting those who wish to come forward and speak their memories of the departed to do so. If possible, it is usually a good idea to have the family of the departed arrange before-hand to have some of the guests prepare to speak to avoid delays or hesitations because no one wants to be first to speak. Once the guests have finished, if the Priest and/or the Priestess knew the departed, they, too, should reflect on their memories of the one who has passed beyond. When the Priest and the Priestess have finished it is time to begin the formal service.

Funerary Service

PRIESTESS: We meet here today in both sadness and in joy. In sadness because a loved and respected friend [*name of the departed*] has left us and we—each in our own way—feel deeply the emptiness left behind by his/her passing.

Yet we also meet in joy in the knowledge that his/her passing signifies that the work of his/her lifetime has reached its time of completion and this time marks for him/her a time of rest and peace in anticipation of new beginnings and new futures as yet untold.

PRIEST: We meet here today to mark [*name of the departed*]'s passing from this incarnation to the care of the God and the Goddess to rest until the time when, once more, he/she will be born again into this world. And, knowing that this is so, we are firm in the knowledge that the sadness and the emptiness we feel at this time will pass—in the compan-ionship of friends and in the life of the world around us—but that the joy of his/her renewal is forever! [Ring the bell three times.] We call to thee, Ama, O dark sterile Mother; thou to whom all manifested life must return when its appointed time has come. Dark Mother of stillness and rest before whom all tremble because they know you not. We call to thee, who art Hecate of the waning moon, Dark Lady of Wisdom whom all fear because Your wisdom over-shadows their own. We, the children of the God and the Goddess, know that there is nothing to fear in Thy embrace,

that when we enter Thy dark realm—as all must—it is not to stay, but only to pass through, once more, until we come again into the world of light.

Therefore in love and without fear do we call upon Thee to commend to Thee our brother/sister [*name of departed*]. Take him/her to You. Guard him/her. Admit him/her to the place of the Summerlands which stands between past life and future life. Take with him/her our love to strengthen him/her upon his/her journey.

PRIESTESS: Listen to the words of the Great Mother who was known to the inner mind of humankind since before the beginning of time. I am the gracious Goddess who gives the gift of joy unto your hearts. Upon earth I give the knowledge of the Spirit Eternal—and beyond death I give peace and freedom—and reunion with those who have gone before. I who am the beauty of the green earth and the silver moon amongst the stars; I who am the mystery of the waters and the desire within the heart of humankind call unto the spirit of [*name of the departed*]. Arise and come unto me for I am the soul of nature who gives life to the universe. From me all things proceed, and unto me all things must return—and before me, beloved of both gods and humankind, thy innermost divine self shall be enfolded in the rapture of the infinite! For behold! I have been with thee from the beginning and I am that which is attained at the end of desire!

PRIEST: If everyone would please stand and take the hand of the person next to you we will come together to form a unity of being and spirit. Now focus your mind on [*name of departed*] as you knew him/her and loved him/her and build your feeling of love to send it forth to enfold and strengthen his/her spirit as he/she continues upon the path of life and more life. [Ring bell nine times.] Let us all be seated once more. [Pause until all are seated.] We call upon Thee, Aima, O bright, fertile Mother. Thou who art the womb of rebirth from whom all life is manifested and at whose flowing breast all are nourished. We call to Thee, Persephone of the waxing moon, Lady of Springtime and of all things renewed. To Thee we commend [*name of departed*], our brother/sister! Take him/her to Thee. Guard him/her. Guide him/her. Bring him/her in the fullness of time to new birth and new life. Grant that in his/her new life he/she may be loved as we his/her brothers and sisters have loved him/her in this life.

PRIESTESS: Hear ye then the words of the Star Goddess. She in the dust of whose feet are the hosts of heaven— whose body encircles the universe. Mine is the ecstasy of the spirit and Mine also is joy on earth—for My law is love unto all beings. Mine is the secret key which opens the door to life and more life. Mine is the cup of the wine of life, the cauldron of Cerridwen—which is the Holy Grail of Immortality! Behold! I am the Gracious Mother who gives birth to those who, like [*name of departed*], in coming to Me would live again. Love is My law, for without love you cannot be born. Love is the binding force of the universe that brings forth all birth. Love is everlasting unto eternity!

PRIEST: Let us now stand. [Pause until all are standing.] As some of us have done so many times in the past with our brother/sister [*name of the departed*] let us share our love with one another. [Priest goes to the Priestess, embraces her and they kiss with an exchange **"Blessed Be, Sister/Brother."** They then go to some of the family and guests and do the exchange with them while encouraging all to do likewise.]

PRIEST [When all have finished]: Let us go from here to [*location of the after service party*] where we will continue to share our love and support with one another while toasting the fond memories of our brother/sister [*name of the departed*].

PRIESTESS: So Mote It Be!

ALL: So Mote It Be!

This service is only one way to conduct a Funerary Rite. When we have used it, the departed, most of the family, and most of the friends who attended the service were pagan, if not Wiccan. Consequently, we did not have to make special allowances for people unfamiliar with the basics of the Wiccan religion. If the immediate family is of the Wiccan religion, but other relatives and friends are of either faiths, it might be a good idea to see if a joint service could be arranged with a priest or minister who is close to the other relatives. If a joint service is not possible, in respect for those attending who are not of the Wiccan religion there are several things that should be done to bring understanding and love forth so that all may be as one.

First, as an opening, the Priest, Priestess, or a family member might begin with: **"[*name of the departed*] was of the Wiccan religion. For those of you here who are unfamiliar with our religion, we believe in a Supreme Force manifested in balanced polarity through the God and the Goddess. Our belief system holds that when we die we are reincarnated and return to continue to learn the lessons life has to offer until such time as we complete those lessons and become one with the Supreme Force of the universe—the force that many religions refer to as God."** You do not need to go into a complete Wicca 101 course. This is not the place for that. However, identifying that Wicca does believe in a God-Force will alleviate some of the apprehension those of other faiths might have. By also mentioning briefly the Wiccan belief in reincarnation, the references to reincarnation in the service will be better understood.

Second, rather than use specific God or Goddess names that would be used in Circle, general references to the God and Goddess are easier to understand for all present.

While some people might regard these considerations as bending to suit Western Christianity, remember that this type of service is not a Wiccan Circle. It is a service intended to remember the departed and to bring all who attend together to share this time in love and companionship. Therefore, working along more commonly understood religious lines rather than specific religious lines will benefit everyone. It is a shame that some other religions, priests, and ministers do not have the same consideration at these times.

As with any of the rituals or services in this book, this Funerary Rite is put forth as a starting point to work from, and it is expected that it will be changed to fit the particular circumstances of different groups or individuals. This rite specifically opens itself to a wide range of change. Work well with it, bring love and strength to those whose need is great.

PART III

CELEBRATING
COVEN TIMES OF CHANGE

One walks a path of Spirit
    To guide one in this life.
In time to join with others
    Finding strength against all strife.
In Wicca these groups, called Covens,
    Are really not that strange.
For they give one self-awareness
    And bring forth Times of Change.

Times that can't be measured
    As to when they will take form.
For all of us are different,
    There really is no norm.
Yet when indeed they happen
    And awareness comes to one,
A gathering is in order
    It's called initiation.

Though all our paths are different,
    Our journeys are the same.
No matter what the calling,
    No matter what the name.
We see, we learn, we grow,
    Our paths we all arrange.
As throughout our lives we celebrate
    All our Times of Change!

CHAPTER 6

AFFIRMING ONE'S PATH

THE WICCAN religion is considered an initiatory religion. That is, Wicca is a religion wherein one periodically goes through initiation ceremonies as one learns more and becomes more aware. This is because Wicca is a religion that seeks to have its members ever strive for new enlightenment and awareness. As each member proceeds along his or her path, they come to realize and understand the lessons that life is presenting each day. Different traditions within the Wiccan religion may have different numbers or levels of initiations, but they all have set degrees of initiation. Some may have three. Some may have, somewhat ceremonially, five—one for each of the elemental levels. Some may have more. The number of initiatory levels only matters to the members of the group. If the number of levels and the reason for each are comfortable to the member, then they are right for that person.

The First Temple of the Craft of W.I.C.A. has basically four initiatory levels—Affirmation, Dedication, First Degree, and Second Degree. In this chapter and the following three chapters, these levels will be discussed, beginning with Affirmation.

When a person comes to the First Temple of the Craft of W.I.C.A. to learn of the Wiccan religion he or she is given a series of classes taught by the Priest and Priestess. The classes begin with an introduction to Wicca, followed by a short history of the Wiccan religion. After these classes, are two serious classes describing and discussing our code of ethics. During these classes a New Moon will occur and the individual will be invited to attend our New Moon celebration as an observer. The student comes to view and feel—not actively participate. At this point the student is still learning of Wicca, still gaining knowledge of the Wiccan religion so that he or she will be able to make an informed choice as to whether Wicca is his or her path or not.

Following the student's attendance at a New Moon celebration, there is a class to discuss and explain what the student observed and felt at the ceremony. Questions that the students may have as to what they saw are answered and we, in turn, ask the students to relate to us what they felt at the ceremony so that we may put those feelings into perspective. By coming to know what feelings the students had during the ceremony, we can get better insight as to whether the Wiccan religion should be the path that they follow. There are those who come to us who are looking for something different that they can be a part of and really do not care whether it is their path so long as they can be part of this different group. For all concerned, it is best to see early that these people are encouraged to look for what they need rather than what they want.

After the class following the New Moon celebration, if the student wishes to continue, there is a class explaining our reasons and ways for celebrating the New and Full Moons as well as the eight festivals that turn the Wheel of Life. This class again stresses the religious importance of each of these times to impress upon the student that Wicca is first and foremost a religion. It is not a Magickal Lodge, nor is Wicca a fast, magickal way to get a girlfriend or boyfriend.

This class is followed by two classes on what a ritual is and how a ritual works. In these classes the student is taught how to construct a basic ritual.

When these classes have been completed, the student is invited by the Priest and Priestess for a serious discussion about his or her intentions for joining the Wiccan religion. If, after completing these classes, the student feels that Wicca may indeed be his or her path, and we feel that the student has been sincere in his or her inner examination, the student is asked to undergo the first initiatory rite, the rite of Affirmation.

Affirmation is just what the title implies. The student affirms that he or she seeks to continue upon the path of Wicca. It is an acknowledgment that the student seeks to learn more of the ways of Wicca and endeavors, in time, to know of the responsibilities that come with this path. It is not a formal Dedication to the path of Wicca with the commitment that dedication would incur. It is, however, a commitment to continued learning and growth.

The following is the Affirmation ritual used by the First Temple of the Craft of W.I.C.A. to open the way for new students. It is presented here in its entirety so that the reader may get a feel for what the ritual is trying to achieve and so that rumors of the "dark practices" of Wicca might be dispelled. While some portions of the ritual may change slightly over time, this is our Affirmation Ritual!

Figure 15. Affirmation Altar set up. You are looking at the altar from where the Priest and Priestess would stand. In addition to the basic altar items, on the pentagram is the candle to be inscribed by the Affirmatant. The small white-handled knife to be used for the inscribing is next to the pentagram. Also on the altar is the Priest's athame (on the left) and the athame of the Priestess (on the right).

Affirmation Ritual

The temple and the altar are arranged as they would be set up for a New Moon Celebration, except instead of a small chalice of anointing oil on the pentacle, there is a white candle large enough for the candidate for Affirmation to engrave his or her name on it. (The candles we use are carried by hardware stores and are called "Plumber's Candles.") A sharp tool to engrave the candle is also on the altar. (See figure 15 on page 85.)

Because the First Temple of the Craft of W.I.C.A. believes in polarity, if the candidate is male, the Priestess shall preside and actually confer Affirmation upon the candidate. If the candidate is female, the Priest presides and actually confers the Affirmation upon the candidate.

In the ritual that follows, the speaking parts for the Priest or Priestess will be indicated by PRIEST/PRIESTESS meaning Priest or Priestess—whoever is actually presiding over the ceremony. There are no parts in this ceremony where both the Priest and the Priestess are speaking together. If we do a multiple Affirmation for several people at the same time—some male and some female—the Priest and the Priestess take turns repeating each part for each person, the Priest conferring the Affirmation upon each female, the Priestess upon each male.

The bell is rung and all are anointed as they enter the Temple. When everyone is in the Temple, the Circle is cast and everyone opens their aura. The Mighty Forces, the God, and the Goddess are then invoked.

PRIEST/PRIESTESS: Come forth, Candidate, and stand before us in the West. [Candidate comes from his or her place in the Circle and goes to stand before the Priest and Priestess in the West facing the altar.] **Do you affirm that you**

seek the path of Light, the path of knowledge of the God and of the Goddess that you might one day be of the Craft of the Wise?

CANDIDATE: I do so affirm!

PRIEST/PRIESTESS: May thy eyes be blessed that they might see the Light!

CANDIDATE: I seek that my eyes might behold the Light.

PRIEST/PRIESTESS: May thy ears be blessed that they might hear the words of Truth!

CANDIDATE: I seek that my ears might hear the words of Truth.

PRIEST/PRIESTESS: May thy mouth be blessed that you might speak the words of Truth!

CANDIDATE: I seek that my mouth might speak the words of Truth.

PRIEST/PRIESTESS: May thy feet be blessed that they might lead you upon your Holy Path!

CANDIDATE: I seek that my feet might walk my Holy Path.

PRIEST/PRIESTESS: May thy heart be blessed that it may be opened to the warmth and love that abounds all around you on your path!

CANDIDATE: I seek that my heart might be opened to the warmth and love that is upon my path.

The Priest/Priestess picks up the white candle and the engraving tool from the altar and holds them before the Candidate.

PRIEST/PRIESTESS: This candle symbolizes the Light—or knowledge—that awaits every person if they find and walk the Holy Path that is theirs and theirs alone. At this time it is unlit and shines no light upon your path or any other for at this time thou art still a seeker searching to find your Holy Path. At such time as you find your Holy Path and Dedicate yourself to walking that path, then, the burning flame of knowledge will shine forth to light your way, burning away all fear and doubt replacing it with love and knowledge.

Take this candle now and upon it inscribe the name that all know you by in the outer world.

The candle is given to the Candidates who inscribe on it the name they go by. For example, someone named Robert might inscribe "Bob" or "Rob" instead of Robert. As the candle will be theirs by virtue of the energy going into it with their work, whether they inscribe their last name is a matter of personal preference left up to the individual group. (See figure 16 on page 90.)

CANDIDATE [When finished inscribing]**: I have done what you have asked.**

PRIEST/PRIESTESS: Take this symbol of yourself that you hold to the altar of the Goddess in the West and, placing it upon Her altar, kneel before Her and ask of Her and Her Consort—the God—what you seek.

CANDIDATE [Goes to the altar of the Goddess in the West and places the candle—unlit—upon the altar and kneels facing West]**: O Mother of All, Creatress of All Living. O Father of the Woodlands, Master of Death and Resurrection. Will you teach [_name of candidate_] that I might learn of Thee and become wise in the love of the Gods? Strong in the aid of humanity? Learned in Thy arts? And skillful in Thy ways?**

PRIEST/PRIESTESS: Seeker of the Path—do you pledge yourself to keep silent of what you shall learn from this time forward and to respect that which is taught you?

CANDIDATE: Gladly do I so pledge myself to keep silent of what I shall now learn and to respect that which is taught me!

PRIESTESS: Then hear, O Candidate, what is laid before thee by the Great Mother, called upon by many names throughout the ages by humankind:
Thou shalt learn of the Mother Earth and of Her ways!
Thou shalt seek harmony with Her through feeling and love!
Thou shalt gather with others and give worship at each New Moon to Me—the Queen of the Heavens!
That if it be ordained in your future to walk the Path of the Craft of the Wise, that you may do so prepared!
Do you understand and shall you work to this end?

CANDIDATE: I do and I shall!

PRIEST: Then hear, O Candidate, what is laid before you by the Consort of our Lady—the Horned One, the Lord of Death and Resurrection:
Thou shalt seek the Path of Light from which all things come!
Thou shalt learn of the Forces of Life and gather with others eight times a year in their celebration!
Thou shalt learn of the ways of the God—to be wise, that in the fullness of time you may be called to my service among those who are called the Mighty Dead! For it is through Me that you shall come to know rebirth—for I am the Lord of Death and Resurrection!
Do you understand and shall you work toward this end?

CANDIDATE: I do and I shall! Blessed be this time that marks my life, that I first set my foot upon the Path of Light, that I begin to learn of the Gods and embrace them as my own!

PRIEST: May the blessings of the Mighty Forces of the Universe go with thee and aid thee on learning of thy path!

PRIESTESS: May the blessings of the Mighty Forces of the Universe go with thee and aid thee on learning of thy path!

PRIEST/PRIESTESS: Take up your candle from the altar of the Goddess. It is yours to keep and care for until such time as you might desire Dedication to the Craft of the Wise. At that time it will play an important part in the ceremony of Dedication. So, again, keep it safe.

The Candidate rises and is kissed and congratulated by the Priest, the Priestess and those in attendance.

The Mighty Forces are dismissed. The auras are closed and the Circle is uncast.

So Mote It Be!

Figure 16. The Affirmatant inscribes her name into the white candle.

In the ritual just described, it is possible to affirm more than one candidate at the same time. In the case of multiple Affirmations, each candidate responds individually and goes before the altar of the Goddess one at a time.

Since Affirmation (like Dedication, First Degree and Second Degree) marks the opening of a new chapter in one's book of life, the ritual should be done as soon as possible after the New Moon so that it takes place during the waxing cycle of the Moon. It should not be done during the waning cycle of the Moon. While it is possible to do the ritual between Samhain and Imbolc—traditionally the time for rest and past reflection rather than forward moves—it is usually best for the student to wait until after Imbolc, or at least until after Yule.

While the First Temple of the Craft of W.I.C.A. will usually have all of its students go through Affirmation, on occasion a student comes to us who has studied with another group or has read extensively and has been practicing Wicca as religion alone as a solitary. In these instances we can, if the situation justifies it, waive the Affirmation ceremony and simply continue with classes.

Once students have gone through the Affirmation ceremony, they are welcome and encouraged to attend the New Moon celebrations as well as the eight Festivals marking the Turning of the Wheel of Life. Then through continued classes and attendance at the New Moon celebrations and Festivals, students get to participate in enough of the Wiccan religion so that they can truly decide whether the Wiccan religion is their personal path. In time, they will be able to knowingly request Dedication to the Craft of the Wise or leave and continue their search for the path that is theirs.

CHAPTER 7

DEDICATING TO THE WICCAN RELIGION

CHRIST, WHEN describing what was to evolve into Christianity, constantly compared the apostles to shepherds. Later, the Priests were also compared to shepherds, and their congregations compared to sheep. The realization here, of course, is based on the fact that most people are sheep and require a shepherd to guide and direct them, or they will run astray.

The Wiccan religion, by contrast, is a religion for the individual. In Wicca we teach our students and will advise our people on personal matters upon request, but for the most part, while we may demonstrate by example and officiate most of the time at rituals, we do not lead those in the coven and we would object greatly if they chose to follow our example blindly without question.

This is why, when people first come to the First Temple of the Craft of W.I.C.A., they are given classes and recommended reading to make them aware of what the Wiccan religion is, what the Wiccan religion believes, and the times and reasons that we meet to celebrate. We have students attend a New Moon celebration to observe and we encourage students to come to Festival celebrations—all before there is any commitment to the Wiccan religion on their part. If they are to join and walk with us, it must be because our path is their path, and the only way for them to truly know of our path is through experiencing it.

After the introduction classes, the students who decide that the Wiccan religion may be the path that they have been searching for, go through the Affirmation ritual which is only a commitment to learn more. While it brings them close enough for us to be comfortable with them at a New Moon celebration, they are still, for the most part, somewhat on the outside looking in—though the view is closer and clearer.

Following the Affirmation Ritual, the students continue with classes to increase their awareness of what we do in our rituals, how we do our rituals, and why we do our rituals. These classes include: Rituals—How and Why They Work; Magickal Correspondences; An Introduction to the Qabbala; and several classes on the Tree of Life. The purpose of this series of classes is to bring the student to an understanding of how the temple members work together in ritual and how, when work of a magickal nature is requested, we set about to do that work. Although for the First Temple of the Craft of W.I.C.A., the religion of Wicca is the primary reason to gather together and any magickal working is incidental to the occasion, magick is still a part of Wicca, and ways of working magick do need to be learned if the student is to be a full part of the coven.

Once students have completed the necessary classes and have attended several New Moon celebrations and a Festival or two, the students will be faced with a serious question that they must ask of themselves—and answer: *Is the Wiccan religion my true path at this point in my life?*

If the answer to this question is no, then we hope that we have contributed to their overall enlightenment and wish them well in their quest for their spiritual path.

If the answer to this question is yes, then they are requested to undergo the Dedication Ritual.

Dedication is a solemn ritual. With this ritual students are undertaking, first, an obligation to do all in their power to bring Wicca into their life as their religion—not just to learn about Wicca, but to live Wicca. Their dedication commits them to a path of learning and living so that, in time, they might grow to become one with the forces and flow of nature—one with the God and the Goddess.

Secondly, through this ritual, the student is dedicating to the Temple. The commitment to the Temple is that for as long as the First Temple of the Craft of W.I.C.A. celebrates the religious occurrences and works its magick, and for as long as the dedicant lives within a reasonable distance of the Temple, and for as long as the dedicant feels comfortable there, the dedicant will attend those religious observances at the First Temple of the Craft of W.I.C.A. and regard it as his or her church. If, for any reason in the future, the dedicant decides to move on to another coven or path, all that is requested is a letter of intent so that we may know of the person's commitment to move away from our specific path.

While one's Dedication to the Wiccan religion should be entered into as a lifetime (or more) commitment to the religion, it is not and should not be regarded as a lifetime commitment to one particular temple or coven. If it turns out that a person does spend a lifetime with one particular temple or coven, it may speak very well of that group; but, by the very makeup of the Wiccan religion with its accent on personal growth and the concept that when people reach a specific level of attained knowledge they are free to "hive off" and form new covens of their own, it is rare for students to stay with their original coven throughout their lifetime unless they have been chosen to replace a coven leader due to illness or old age.

As the Dedication Ritual signifies a time of new beginnings, the ritual should be done as soon as possible after a New Moon. In some covens—like the First Temple of the Craft of W.I.C.A.—Dedications are not performed during the reign of the Crone, between Samhain and Imbolc.

Since dedication *is* a serious step for the student, the student should be encouraged to talk out any questions or fears about dedication with the Priest or Priestess beforehand. Once accepted, the Dedication Ritual should be free of any energies that might lessen its true meaning for the student being dedicated. The student being dedicated should be given a copy of the Dedication Ritual to read through thoroughly before the ceremony.

Though the Dedication Ritual is a solemn one, the time following it *is* a time of joy, for the student has become a dedicant and is now a member of the Craft of the Wise! The time immediately following the ritual is a time for celebration. As such, plans should be made with those attending to bring food and drink so that after the ritual there may be a feast of celebration and welcome or, if the Dedication Ritual is done later in the evening, a party of welcome for the new Dedicant.

What follows is the Dedication Ritual used by the First Temple of the Craft of W.I.C.A. for many years. Through time some of the invocations and charges may have changed slightly or may have been added to, but the core of the ritual has remained constant throughout its use.

Figure 17. Dedication altar set up. You are looking at the altar from where the Priest and the Priestess would stand. For this ritual, in addition to the basic altar items, there is the candle that the candidate inscribed when Affirmed, a small candle that will be used for divination, and the quartz crystal star that will be the symbol of his or her dedication to the First Temple of the Craft of W.I.C.A. Also on the altar is the athame of the Priest (on the left) and the athame of the Priestess (on the right).

Dedication Ritual

In addition to the usual altar set up, include a small candle (like a birthday cake candle) for use in a divination during the ritual, a quartz crystal star on a silver chain—the new dedicant's outward symbol of becoming a part of the First Temple of the Craft of W.I.C.A., and the white candle that the student was given at the Affirmation Ritual on which he or she inscribed his or her name. The divination candle, quartz crystal star, and the inscribed white candle are all on the altar. (See figure 17 on page 96.)

The inscribed white candle for the Dedication Ritual is used to symbolize two things: 1) when lit, the candle represents the Light of Knowledge burning brightly for the new dedicant; 2) as it burns, the candle melts away the dedicant's given name in favor of his or her new chosen "witch's name" by which he or she will be known in the Circle when he or she works magick. The melting signifies the death of the "old" person and the "birth" of the new dedicant into the Wiccan religion.

As in the Affirmation Ritual, to maintain polarity, if the student is male, the Priestess presides over the ritual and is the one who actually acknowledges the dedication of the student. If the student is female, then the Priest is the one who presides and acknowledges the dedication of the student.

In the ritual that follows the speaking part of the person presiding over the ritual will be shown as "PRIEST/PRIEST-ESS," meaning Priest or Priestess. There are no parts in the ritual where both the Priest and the Priestess are speaking together. If a multiple dedication—including both males and females—is being performed, the Priest and the Priestess take turns, the Priest repeating each part for each female dedicant, and the Priestess doing the same for each male dedicant.

The bell is rung and all are anointed as they enter the Temple. When everyone is in the Temple, the Circle is cast and everyone opens their aura. The Mighty Forces are invoked, as are the God and the Goddess.

PRIEST/PRIESTESS [To the dedicant]: **Do you wish to be dedicated to the God and to the Goddess that you may learn of Them and that you may join the Craft of the Wise?**

DEDICANT: I do! Blessed are my eyes that have seen this day!

PRIEST/PRIESTESS: Blessed indeed are thy eyes!

DEDICANT: Blessed are my ears that have heard the words of truth!

PRIEST/PRIESTESS: Blessed indeed are thy ears!

DEDICANT: Blessed is my mouth that it may speak of the blessings of the God and the Goddess!

PRIEST/PRIESTESS: Blessed indeed is thy mouth!

DEDICANT: Blessed are my feet that have led me onto my path, the Path of Light!

PRIEST/PRIESTESS: Blessed indeed are thy feet!

DEDICANT: Blessed is my heart that has been opened to the warmth and love of those that surround me on this path!

PRIEST/PRIESTESS: Blessed indeed is thy heart!

PRIEST/PRIESTESS [Picking up the small divination candle]: **Dedicant, take this candle, light it and stand it upon the altar. Know that as it burns down, by its flame and direction it will reveal to those here knowledge of your future upon the path you have chosen this day.**

The dedicant takes the small divination candle, lights it and places it on the altar to burn down. If there are more than two people who are dedicating, wait to light the divination candles until after the charge of the God.

PRIEST/PRIESTESS [Picks up the inscribed white candle]: **This candle symbolizes the light—or knowledge—that awaits every person that finds and walks their Holy Path, the path that they find within themselves. Take this candle and light it that it may shine forth its radiance upon your path! Once lit, place it upon the altar of the Goddess in the west. Let it shine your way to Her before you. As it burns— and by so burning erases the outer shell by which you came here— reflect within upon the name that She and Her Consort will forever know you by and speak it softly to Her. Then, aloud, speak from your heart.**

Dedicant takes the candle, lights it and goes to the altar in the west and places the candle there. Kneeling, the dedicant chooses a Craft name. (See figure 18 on page 102.)

DEDICANT [Facing west, to the Goddess]: **O Mother of All, Creatress of all that lives.**
     O Father of the woodlands and Consort of my Lady, O Lord of Death and Resurrection.
     Hear me now! I am here—a simple Pagan—holding Thee and Thy ways in reverence and honor.
     Far have I journeyed and long have I searched to find the path that will lead me to that which I hold most dear.
     I seek to be one with the trees and with the fields.
     I seek to be one with the woods and with the springs.
     I seek to be one with the streams and with the lakes.
     I seek to be one with the heavens and with the stars.
     I seek to be one with Thee—and Thee one with me!
     Grant me that which I desire! Grant me that which is my will!
     Permit me to join the Craft of the Wise and give worship to the Gods and all that the Gods represent!
     Make me a lover of the Life that is within all things!
     Love IS the Law! Love under Will!

PRIEST/PRIESTESS: Beloved, do you pledge yourself to the Goddess, to love and honor Her; and to the Horned God, to love and honor Him?

DEDICANT: Gladly do I so pledge myself—to the Goddess, to love and honor Her; and to the Horned God, to love and honor Him!

PRIEST/PRIESTESS: Beloved, do you pledge to keep silent of that which you shall learn from this time forward and to respect that which is taught you?

DEDICANT: Gladly do I so pledge myself, to keep silent of what I shall now learn and to respect that which is taught me!

PRIESTESS: Then hear now the charge of the Great Mother, who of old was called among men—Isis, Artemis, Astarte, Diana, Aphrodite, and many other names, some so old as to be lost to consciousness. Before whose altars all the world approached in love and reverence!

I AM the eternal Goddess! Yet, I demand no sacrifice. Rather I give to those who would honor me!

Yet, I charge thee, that if you would be Mine and follow in My ways—

You shall gather once at each New and Full Moon and give worship to Me—your Queen.

To you will I teach that which is yet unknown.

For mine is the secret that opens upon the door of youth eternal, mine is the Cup of the wine of Life and the Cauldron of Cerridwen, which IS the Holy Grail of Immortality!

I am the gracious Goddess who gives the gift of joy unto the hearts of all on Earth.

Each must recognize Me and look at Me lest you forget from whom you come and to whom you are called.

If you would be mine, you must honor My charge, for those things which I have made Law may be dissolved by no person!

Shall you obey My charge?

DEDICANT: Gladly shall I obey the Charge of the Goddess!

PRIEST: Hear ye then the Charge of the God!

I AM the Light from which all things do come and without which nothing can exist. The rays of My existence bring life and hope to all of humankind!

Many Gods bear My name, but to you My name is that of Love. And when you call upon Me, I shall come to you in this form!

In My honor and that of My Duality you shall gather eight times a year in celebration of the Turning of the Wheel of Life.

You shall be taught to be wise and to receive My knowledge that in the fullness of time you may be counted among those who are near to Me in My service—among those who are called the Mighty Dead!

For it is through Me that you are born again. I AM the Lord of Death and Resurrection! It is through Me that you shall gain Eternal Life!

Do you understand and shall you obey My Charge?

DEDICANT: To the best of my will do I understand Your Charge and gladly shall I obey it!

PRIEST/PRIESTESS [Picking up the red Fire candle and holding it before the Dedicant]: Then hold your hands over the Sacred Flame and repeat after me:

I dedicate myself to the Path of Light!
May I always walk in the Light.
Live, love, and have by being.
Knowing that which I seek, I shall attain!

(See figure 18 on page 103.)

DEDICANT: Blessed be this time that marks my path in life, that I shall ever after be a child of the Gods, that I shall learn of Them and embrace Them as my own.

Ever will I revere Them and protect that which is
Theirs.
Let none speak ill of Thee, for ever will I defend Thee.
You are my life and I am Yours from this day forth.
So Mote It Be!

ALL: So Mote It Be!

PRIEST [Stands before the Dedicant and makes an earth
invoking pentagram in the aura of the Dedicant]: **May the
blessings of the Mighty Forces of the Universe be ever
with thee!**

PRIESTESS [Stands before the Dedicant and makes an earth
invoking pentagram in the aura of the Dedicant]: **May the
blessings of the Mighty Forces of the Universe be ever
with thee!**

PRIEST/PRIESTESS [Picking up the quartz crystal star]:
**This crystal star is the outward sign that you are a part of
the First Temple of the Craft of W.I.C.A. and are now welcome at all of our gatherings that are pertinent to your
degree level. It is not yours to keep—merely to care for. As
you have been taught, your dedication is to this Temple only
so long as it is comfortable to your path. If the time comes
that you would seek to move on to another coven or group,
we would seek the return of this crystal star. Until that
time would occur—if it ever does—wear this crystal star at
all ritual times, whether with the group or by yourself. At
those times that you would work rituals of a personal
nature by yourself know that through this crystal star you
are connected to the energies of the group and can draw
upon them for your work if the need arises.** [The crystal star
is placed around the neck of the Dedicant. See figure 18 on
page 103.]

The Dedicant is hugged, kissed, and congratulated by everyone in the Circle. Everyone then sits and watches the div-

Figure 18. Top: The dedicant kneeling before the Goddess altar in the West pledging her devotion to the Goddess and the God while the inscribed candle burns down before her. Middle: "I dedicate myself to the path of light! May I always walk in the light. Live, love and have by being, knowing that which I seek I shall attain!" Bottom: The new dedicant receives the symbol of her dedication to the temple.

Figure 19. Top: At first, the divination candle is lit and burning for all to see. (The divination candle is sitting on the pentagram.) The candle burns with a tall, straight, intense flame. Then we see the divination candle burned down over halfway (in a short time). The candle burns with a tall, straight, intense flame. This signifies the dedicant is motivated by an intense drive, nearly all-consuming, unwavering from his or her true path. Next, the candle has all but burned away, and yet, it still burns with a tall, intense flame. This dedicant will draw on the power of fire to continue on the path when others would fall away. The photo at the bottom shows all that is left—a small amount of ash. The candle has burned fiercely and completely. This dedicant will work through his or her karmic lessons in this life and not carry forward a karmic debt.

ination candle as it burns down and out to see what insights, direction, and guidance it provides. Anyone who feels they have a message for the Dedicant from the divination candle gives their message. (See figure 19 on page 104.) When everyone is finished, the Mighty Forces are dismissed. The God and the Goddess are thanked. The auras are closed and the Circle is uncast.

So Mote It Be!

Dedication marks the formal acceptance of the Wiccan religion as one's personal path in life with all the responsibilities that the Wiccan religion carries. After the Dedication Ritual, the dedicant is now expected to join with the coven at its Full Moon celebrations, as well as its New Moon and Festival celebrations. In addition, the new dedicant joins with the rest of the coven in the ongoing classes offered by the Temple in topics ranging from various forms of divination to in-depth classes on the Qabbala and aspects of Ceremonial Magick.

All in all, the continuing classes are intended to open the new dedicant so that he or she may, in time, be able to make full use of their inner abilities. As the Wiccan religion attempts to bring the individual into awareness and harmony with the various cycles of life, so are these classes intended to assist in that overall development. In addition, the classes help the dedicant to prepare for his or her eventual advancement to First Degree.

Dedication is the first step on a new spiritual path.

CHAPTER 8

FIRST DEGREE INITIATION

THE FIRST Temple of the Craft of W.I.C.A. does not believe in an elaborate multi-level degree system, which to us, is more indicative of a Magickal Lodge than of a religion. Within the First Temple of the Craft of W.I.C.A., once a person is dedicated, there are only two degree initiation levels—First Degree and Second Degree, although the second degree level does have two variations. These degree initiations are formal recognition of the individual's attainment to a particular level of awareness and ability. In this chapter, the First Degree initiation will be discussed. The Second Degree Initiation will be discussed in the following chapter.

What is First Degree? Or, more properly, what does a First Degree Initiation represent?

As dedicants continue their classes with us, they are opened to a broad spectrum of knowledge. Some of the knowledge in these classes is very pertinent to each dedicant's personal path. Other classes introduce areas of knowledge that the dedicant may have no real interest in, but will still broaden the dedicant's base of information.

Topics intended to bring the dedicant to a First Degree level include: forms of divination; the Qabalah and the Tree of Life; the construction of rituals; mythology and Wicca; reincarnation, karma, and the Wiccan code of ethics; several of the occult sciences.

Classes on the various forms of divination cover the basics of the Tarot, Rune Stones, and the I-Ching, just to name a few. Through these classes, the dedicants are able to choose from the different forms of divination the ones that interest them and, by working with the forms of divination, find the particular form that works best for them. If the dedicant has worked with a form of divination in the past, these classes expose the dedicant to other forms of divination that the dedicant may have been curious about, but never had the opportunity to try. Through the use of any of the methods of divination, the intuitive side of the dedicant is opened. This opening of the dedicant's inner intuitive nature is one of the prerequisites to reaching the level of First Degree. A First Degree Initiate *is* a person who has contact with his or her inner voice and is able to call upon that inner voice for self-guidance and direction or for help for others when the need arises.

Classes on the Qabalah and the Tree of Life are also part of the dedicant's introduction to Wicca. As we use some of the Qabbalistic exercises for personal balance and for Magick, dedicants are expected to acquire enough knowledge of the Tree of Life and the Qabbalistic system to participate in these exercises comfortably. By their very nature, some of these exercises open the person's awareness to some of the intangible yet ever present forces that surround us every day. Once we are aware of these forces, we can learn how to work with them to bring ourselves into closer harmony with nature. A First Degree Initiate is a person who is capable of using these Qabbalistic exercises to achieve the balance of will necessary to walk his or her path in harmony with nature.

Classes on the construction of rituals are offered for new dedicants. All members of the coven are valued for their input into the rituals that we do—not only for their energy in the Circle, but also for their ideas on ways to make a ritual more meaningful or more effective. In order for our members to fully appreciate the intricacies in ritual creation, we sit down and go through various rituals so that they will first understand the basic outline that is used for almost all of the rituals done by the First Temple of the Craft of W.I.C.A. (as well as most other groups). This background allows the dedicant to then take the outline and fill in the details to begin to create rituals of his or her own. Secondly, by going over various rituals we show the work we seek to accomplish through a particular ritual and discuss how we make the ritual actually accomplish that work. As part of their ongoing education, the dedicants are first given a New Moon ritual to officiate as the Priest or the Priestess. Once the dedicant has experienced handling and controlling the energies of this ritual, at a subsequent New Moon ritual they will not only be asked to officiate, but they will also be asked to determine in what way any magick needed should be worked. If the dedicant has a new chant or a different type of visualization that might be used for doing magick, at this ritual the dedicant is free to use it. At a later class the ritual is discussed and the other members who were in Circle are asked for their feelings regarding the changes made by the dedicant who was officiating. It is emphasized at the class that there is no right or wrong connected with the critique which is only a discussion of how it felt to the group. A First Degree Initiate is a person who can help create and work an effective ritual.

Classes on various mythologies are held. When we stand in Circle we call out to Ra, Apollo, Cerridwen, Astarte, and many other Gods and Goddesses. Do we really know who they are and what their attributes or powers are? Through several classes the First Temple of the Craft of W.I.C.A. explores the various myths referred to most often and the Gods and Goddesses connected with those myths. The dedicant is educated to understand why we call to a particular God or Goddess when we work in a specific area so that the dedicant will be comfortable and knowledgeable when standing in Circle and using the name of a God or Goddess. A First Degree Initiate is a person who is able to call upon the Gods and the Goddesses because they know Them.

Classes on reincarnation, karma, and the ethics connected therein are also important. Wicca is a religion and, as such, has a very rigorous code of ethics: *"Do what thou Wilt is the whole of the Law!"* While some groups may add an addendum such as *"an ye harm none,"* the basic code does say it all. What most people fail to realize is that there is a world of difference between will and want. The dedicant is given classes explaining that difference along with the karmic repercussions all actions create and their effects on reincarnation and future lives. The First Degree Initiate is a person who understands the Law and works to live by his or her will.

Classes on several of the occult sciences including the aura, herbs, astrology, and astral projection are given. The dedicant is encouraged through these classes to come to a better understanding of each of the various areas of knowledge that can be of great use both personally on a specific path in life as well as for others if called upon to aid another in walking his or her path of life. For some of these topics the classes are in depth, hands on, relatively full explanations/instructions that enable the dedicant to go from the class and begin to work within the particular area. For other topics, the classes are meant merely to expose the dedicant to the topic, giving just an introduction and the basics so that the dedicant will be aware of the topic. If the individual is interested, reading material to further his or her knowledge is recommended. If the interest extends to several members of the Temple, an in-depth class on the topic will be scheduled. As there is such a variety of subject matter that might be explored through classes, there is, of course, a limitation on how many topics will be discussed in depth. Yet, we realize that the needs of every individual are different, and we would not wish to hinder anyone by keeping him or her from a topic that may be personally instrumental to attaining the goal of First Degree. A First Degree Initiate is a person who has a basic knowledge of many of the occult sciences, a thorough understanding of several of them, and a constant desire to learn more.

In summary, for dedicants to reach the level of awareness and balance that is necessary to be recognized as First Degree Initiates within the First Temple of the Craft of W.I.C.A., they must have basic knowledge in several of the occult sciences such as herb craft, astrology, and astral projection. They need to be capable of assisting in the creation of rituals as well as able to raise and control energy within the ritual. They must have a broad knowledge of the various mythologies that are drawn upon in ritual and a good knowledge of the specific mythos most used by the Temple. They need to be completely cognizant of the annual cycle we work with in the Turning of the Wheel and be working toward bringing their lives into harmony with that cycle. They must be somewhat skilled in one of the methods of divination and conversant with several others. Last—and most important—they need to understand fully the ethics of the Wiccan religion and to strive to live their lives by those ethics.

When an individual has met these criteria as determined by observation, a minimal amount of testing, and the gut feeling of the Priest and the Priestess, the individual will be approached and asked if he or she is ready for First Degree initiation. The individual will be asked to respond in writing. After reviewing the response, the Priest and Priestess will go over it with the dedicant. First Degree initiation is not taken lightly.

The Temple acknowledges and our classes teach that everyone's path in life is different. No two people proceed through life at the same pace, and no two people's goals in life are exactly the same. It may well be that an individual comes to the Temple, dedicates, and a serious year later has shown all the qualifications to receive a First Degree initiation. For others it may take two years, three years, or even a lifetime before they achieve the level of First Degree. Like any journey in life, it is not the destination, but the trip itself that is important. Those who put the achievement of the First Degree level before them as a goal, concentrating on learning all that there is to know to the exclusion of all else, will reach their goal far behind those who see First Degree as simply incidental to living a good, balanced life.

The following is the ritual for First Degree initiation as used by the First Temple of the Craft of W.I.C.A. While portions of it may change in time, its essence will not. The ritual is full and complete. Nothing has been left out. There may be those who, upon seeing the ritual presented with such completeness, will scream that the oath of secrecy has been violated. They should note first that the ritual is an acknowledgment of a level of awareness already achieved, though in some cases not fully realized by the individual. Secondly, every First Degree initiation is a personal experience! The ritual that follows is just comprised of printed words in a book. For those who are not truly ready but go through the ritual, the end result will be little more than just reading words in a book. They will not experience the opened awareness that the ritual performed appropriately should achieve.

First Degree Initiation Ritual

The candidates for First Degree are placed in an area separate from the Temple to meditate on the degree they are about to receive. The room is dark or lit by a single candle. If so desired, quiet meditation music may be playing. The candidates are robed—but the robes are loose and not corded. They are blindfolded.

The Temple area is set up in much the same way as it is for a Full Moon ritual, though on the altar there are no cakes,

Figure 20. First Degree Initiation altar set up. You are looking at the altar from where the Priest and Priestess would stand. In addition to the basic altar items, there is a chalice of wine or juice and a white cord 4-1/2 feet long. The athame of the Priest is on the left and the athame of the Priestess is on the right.

only a chalice of wine or juice. Also on the altar is a white cord, 4-$\frac{1}{2}$ feet long[1]. (See figure 20 on page 112.)

For this ritual, in addition to the Priest and the Priestess, four attendants are needed—one designated for each of the Quarters (East, South, West, and North) to challenge the candidates. A summoner is also needed to bring the candidates into the Circle at the proper time and guide them on their "journey." If the coven is small, the Priest may act as summoner and two people may alternate the parts of the Quarters.

The bell is rung and all are anointed as they enter the Temple. When everyone is in the Temple, the Circle is cast and everyone opens their aura. The Mighty Forces are invoked as are the God and the Goddess.

Then the Priestess goes to the northeast and creates a doorway in the Circle. The summoner goes forth to bring the candidates—still blindfolded—to the Circle.

While the summoner goes out to bring the candidates to the Circle, the people representing the four Quarters take their places in the respective quarters, with the North Challenger taking from the altar the anointing oil, the West Challenger taking from the altar the chalice of wine or juice, the South Challenger taking from the altar the Fire candle, and the East Challenger taking from the altar the censer and incense.

When the summoner returns with the candidates, they are brought—still blindfolded—to just inside the edge of the Circle. The Priestess closes the doorway previously constructed.

---

[1] The cord is used to belt the robe around the waist. It also has another practical use. The standard working circle is 9 feet in diameter. The cord is 4-$\frac{1}{2}$ feet long—the radius of a 9 foot diameter circle. One end of the cord can be pinned down, say in the woods for an outdoor ritual, and with the athame on the other end, a person can inscribe a 9 foot circle in the ground. However, some groups use a 9 foot cord with the midpoint pinned down to help inscribe a working circle.

PRIEST: You stand in darkness at the edge of light. Before you continue open your aura to the energies that will be.

The candidates open their auras. The candidates are led clockwise around the outer edge of the Circle to the North.

NORTH CHALLENGER [Holding the anointing oil]: You stand in the North, the place of greatest darkness—yet it *is* the doorway to the gate of Light. What brings thee here?

CANDIDATES: I travel the path in search of the Light!

NORTH CHALLENGER: What passwords do you bring?

CANDIDATES: Perfect Love and Perfect Trust!

NORTH CHALLENGER: I, guardian of the watchtower of the North, must forbid thee entrance. You cannot enter this holy place from the North, lest you first be purified and consecrated!
　　Child of Darkness—Seeker of the Light, stand now firm in thy quest and be anointed and blessed that you may continue ever forward and enter this holy place!" [North Challenger takes the anointing oil and anoints each Candidate's forehead with the sign of the Earth Invoking pentagram. When finished, the oil is placed back on the altar. See figure 21 on page 122.]

The candidates are led clockwise around the Circle to the West.

WEST CHALLENGER [Holding the chalice of wine or juice]: You stand in the West, cool and flowing, inviting you to stay. The waters of the West you must pass over if you would seek the gate of Light. What brings thee here?

CANDIDATES: I travel the path in search of the Light!

WEST CHALLENGER: What passwords do you bring?

CANDIDATES: Perfect Love and Perfect Trust!

WEST CHALLENGER: I, guardian of the watchtower of the West, must forbid thee entrance. You cannot enter this holy place from the West, lest you first be purified and consecrated!

Child of Darkness—Seeker of the Light, stand now firm in thy quest and partake of the sacred waters that you may continue forward refreshed into this holy place!" [West Challenger takes the chalice of wine or juice and gives the Candidates a drink. When finished, the chalice is placed back on the altar. See figure 21 on page 122.]

The candidates are led clockwise around the Circle to the South.

SOUTH CHALLENGER [Holding the Fire candle]**: You stand in the South, before the Fire of Life—the Fire that creates by consuming all! You must pass through this wall of fire if you would continue your search for the gate of Light. What brings thee here?**

CANDIDATES: I travel the path in search of the Light!

SOUTH CHALLENGER: What passwords do you bring?

CANDIDATES: Perfect Love and Perfect Trust!

SOUTH CHALLENGER: I, guardian of the watchtower of the South, must forbid thee entrance. You cannot enter this holy place from the South, lest you first be purified and consecrated!

Child of Darkness—Seeker of the Light, stand now firm in thy quest and, holding forth thy hands, be warmed by the sacred fire that you may continue forward to the holy place purified by the Fire of Life! [South Challenger holds the fire candle beneath the candidates' outstretched hands taking care not to burn them. When finished, the Fire candle is placed back on the altar. See figure 21 on page 122.]

The candidates are led clockwise around the Circle to the East.

EAST CHALLENGER [Holding the censer and incense]: **You stand in the East, the breath of life in air can make one's head spin and reel so that one loses direction and bearing. If you are seeking the gate of Light you must keep your senses and direction. What brings thee here?**

CANDIDATES: I travel the path in search of the Light!

EAST CHALLENGER: What passwords do you bring?

CANDIDATES: Perfect Love and Perfect Trust!

EAST CHALLENGER: I, guardian of the watchtower of the East, must forbid thee entrance. You cannot enter this holy place from the East, lest you first be purified and consecrated!

 Child of Darkness—Seeker of the Light, stand now firm in thy quest and partake of the breath of life so that you may continue forward to the holy place purified! [East Challenger takes the censer and inscribes an Air Invoking pentagram into the aura of the candidates. When finished, the censer and incense are placed back on the altar. See figure 21 on page 122.]

The candidates are led clockwise around the Circle to the northeast corner of the Circle where the Priestess stands ready with the sword from the altar. She places the tip of the sword to the throat of each candidate in turn.

PRIESTESS: Do you, who have traveled so far upon the path seeking the gate of Light, have the courage to take but one more final step forward?

CANDIDATES: I do!

PRIESTESS: To serve the Goddess and the God and to give Them reverence?

CANDIDATES: I do!

PRIESTESS: To guard that which is shown to you from the unworthy?

CANDIDATES: I do!

PRIESTESS: For I say to you verily it would be better to rush upon my weapon and perish than to take this step with fear or doubt in thy heart! Do you have the passwords?

CANDIDATES: Perfect Love and Perfect Trust!

PRIESTESS: All who come forth with these words in their heart are doubly welcome! [Priestess lowers sword.] When we enter the world of humankind at birth we do so through woman by force thrust forth against form. . .by that same means do you enter this world now!

The Priestess uses her body and hands to push the candidate into the Circle where he or she is caught by Temple members standing inside the Circle. After all the candidates are in the Circle, the Priestess replaces the sword on the altar.

PRIEST: O thou who hast traveled the path and hath found the gate of Light, hear now that which thou must know— and realize in thy heart!
Of one is the race of humankind and of Gods. From a single source do we both draw our life essence—but a difference in power in everything does keep us apart. For, we are as nothing in the full span of time, yet, the Gods are forever.

However, we can—in Wisdom—be like the Gods! Though we know not to what goal by the light of day or in the darkness of night we might be called, Fate has written that we shall run beyond all seas, and beyond Earth's last boundaries.

Beyond the spring of night and the Heaven's vast expanse there lies a majesty which is the domain of the Gods. Those who would pass through the gates of Night and Day to that great place which lies between the world of humankind and the realms of the Mighty Ones must first know that unless there is truth in their beings and love in their hearts, their every effort is doomed to failure!

PRIESTESS: Hear you, then, the Law!

Thou shall love all the things that exist in nature!

Thou shall suffer no person, nor animal to be unjustly harmed by thy hands or in thy mind!

Thou shall walk humbly in the ways of humankind and in the ways of the Gods!

Thou shall learn—through suffering, if need be—from length of years and from nobility of mind, and through firmness of purpose!

For the wise never grow old! Their minds are nourished by living in the daylight of the Gods!

Now go to the West and kneel before the altar of the Goddess and Her Consort!

The Candidates go to the West and kneel. The Priest sounds the gong slowly eleven times.

PRIEST/PRIESTESS [For the fivefold kiss, the Priest speaks to and kisses female candidates, the Priestess speaks to and kisses male candidates to maintain polarity]: Rise! In some religions the postulant kneels as the Priest claims supreme power, but in the Craft of the Wise we are taught to be humble to one another and, so, I prostrate myself before thee and say:

Blessed be thy feet that walk the path of Light! [Priest/Priestess kisses the candidate's feet. See figure 22 on page 123.]

Blessed be thy knees, that shall kneel at the sacred altar in service to the Lord and the Lady! [Priest/Priestess kisses the candidate's knees.]

Blessed is thy groin [for male] **womb** [for female], **without which we would not be!** [Priest/Priestess kisses the candidate's groin or womb.]

Blessed be thy breasts, formed in beauty and in strength! [Priest/Priestess kisses the candidate's breasts.]

Blessed be thy lips, which shall utter the sacred names! [Priest/Priestess kisses the candidate's lips.]

PRIESTESS: Art thou ready to swear to be true to the Craft of the Wise and to follow in its ways?

CANDIDATES: Yes, I am and I do!

Priest sounds gong slowly seven times.

PRIESTESS [Picking up the cord for the candidates from the altar]: **In some religions, symbols and badges of authority are flourished in pomp and circumstance with their bright colors and trappings so that all may see and be awed. In the Craft of the Wise this** [holds up the cord] **is your mark of recognition,** [ties one small knot in each end of the cord] **and these small knots are your badge of authority. If you are not known well for your wisdom and your deeds, then all the colors in the rainbow and all the costuming that money can buy will avail you not. Wear them well with pride as you walk your path.** [Priest/Priestess cord the dedicants. See figure 22 on page 123.]

PRIEST: Know you then that from this day forward you walk in the service of the Lady of the Moon and the Lord of Death and Resurrection.

Know that in the Universe every form of being, every form of life is connected—one with one another—and that all contain the divine essence.

Harmonize with the forces of Nature, celebrate the Turning of the Wheel of Life with seasonal ritual and direct these forces for your own growth and for the growth of others in accordance with your will.

Know that it is the honoring of Nature and the honoring of the Gods that makes you become more fully one with the Universe.

The coven joins hands around the dedicants to dance and chant.

ALL: Eko, eko, Azurak; Eko, eko, Zomelak; Eko, eko, Aradas; Eko, eko, Cernunnos! [Repeat at least three times—more if the energy feels real good.]

The Priestess picks up the chalice from the altar, holds it before the candidates and places each candidate's hands around it.

PRIESTESS: By the cauldron of Cerridwen, in the name of the Lady and those covenanted to Her, in the name of the Lord of Death and Resurrection and those in His service, I place this threefold charge upon you: To grow to know the Goddess and the God; By so knowing, to love the Goddess and the God; Through that knowledge and love advance in the Craft of the Wise to serve the Ancient Ones!

Do you freely accept this charge?

CANDIDATES: I do!

The candidates' blindfolds are removed by the Priest and Priestess.

PRIEST: We welcome you to the way of the Ancient Ones, to the fold of the Olde Religion, into the house of the Pagans, and into the Craft of the Wise.

Hear you our charge!

Your first duty is that which you have sworn to above, but there is another Law and it is: *Do what thou wilt—with love!*

Do you accept this law and swear to live by it?

CANDIDATES: I do and I shall!

PRIESTESS: Then we welcome you into our midst!

The group congratulates the new initiates with hugs and kisses.

The Mighty Forces are dismissed. The God and the Goddess are thanked. Everyone closes their aura and the Circle is uncast.

So Mote It Be!

Like the dedication ritual, the First Degree initiation ritual marks an individual's attainment of a new level of awareness and development. Therefore, it is a celebration! Once the formal ritual has been completed, it is a time to party. In planning the First Degree initiation, arrange for people attending to bring refreshments to share after the ritual.

By receiving the First Degree initiation, individuals mark a time on their paths where their awareness and knowledge has been noted by others around them. While the notice gives a momentary "high," the individual should be aware that this moment is simply a mile marker on the highway of life. It is not, nor should it be, their final destination. Life at its greatest is a never ending experience in learning. Some of the lessons might be called trivial, others monumental insights, but all of them, lived one at a time and the meaning of each realized by the initiate, make for a life well lived.

For some, receiving the First Degree initiation will mark the beginning of a time of living life for its meaning with continued classes and learning in the subjects closest to the individual's personal likes. It may well be the individual's path

Figure 21. Top: The candidate is purified with oil by the Guardian of the North. Next: The candidate is purified by the Cup of Cerridwen by the Guardian of the West. Then, the candidate is purified with the fire by the Guardian of the South. Bottom: The Candidate is purified by the element of Air by the Guardian of the East.

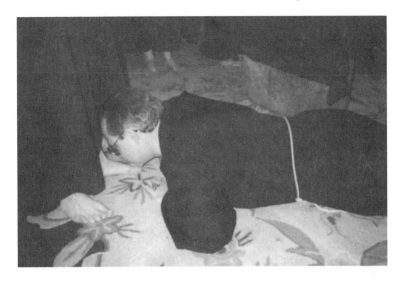

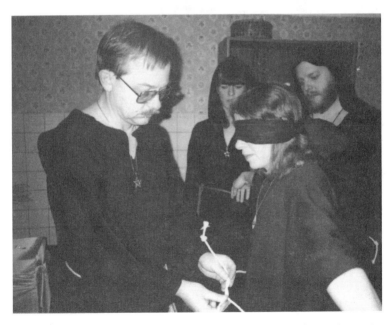

Figure 22. Top: "And so I prostrate myself before thee and say [Priest kisses the Candidate's feet]: Blessed be thy feet that walk the Path of Light!" Bottom: The Candidate is corded with the badge of the First Degree Initiate used by the First Temple of the Craft of W.I.C.A. Note the single knot tied at the end of the cord.

to grow little beyond the level marked by the First Degree initiation. Considering the level of development marked by a First Degree initiation, this is an achievement in itself. For others, their First Degree initiation marks a brief rest on a continuing quest for knowledge and growth that may, in time, lead them onward to receiving a Second Degree initiation.

CHAPTER 9

THE PREREQUISITES FOR SECOND DEGREE INITIATION

THE LEGEND of the Grail is told to all those who seek Second Degree Initiation. Listen as the High Priest relates the story of one of his seekers:

Listen now, you who would aspire to leadership within the Craft of the Wise, to a tale. It is the Legend of the Grail, which is also known to us as the Cauldron of Cerridwen.

In a time long ago a once valiant knight—driven on now by shame and guilt for thoughtless deeds done for ego and greed—while traveling through a forgotten forest happened upon an old, old castle which had the appearance of being abandoned. As night was fast approaching and being in need of shelter, the knight entered the castle. The aura of the old castle mystified the knight. Seeking to satisfy his curiosity and mayhap line his near empty purse, the knight set about to explore the castle. From room to room he went seeing little of any consequence, merely drab, forgotten furnishings. Growing weary he vowed to examine only one more room and then go back and retire for the evening.

With a heavy sigh—already knowing in his heart that he would find only disappointment—he opened the last door and entered the room. He could not believe his eyes. The room was regally decorated with tapestries of black and gold. The floor he walked on shimmered beneath his feet—a moving mosaic of iridescent stone. He looked up and for a moment mistook the high vaulted ceiling for an opening looking out upon the evening sky. It was painted a midnight blue speckled with stars of gold and silver. Trembling with awe, he looked around. Before him in the center of the room was a gilded table. On the table was an object covered with a white silk cloth. Around the object light shifted, jumped, and moved as if it were dancing to some silent music being played by mighty magic forces.

The once valiant knight trembled with fear. He knew that this was a sacred place of old, old Gods who had immense power. This was not a place for mere mortals like himself.

Suddenly in the doorway a tall, old figure appeared—the Grail King!

The knight driven by fear and his guilt for violating so sacred a place, rushed to the doorway and in the panic of those fears struck down the old Grail King.

The Gods of old and the powers incumbent in the room blazed in anger at this sacrilege thus committed. Mighty forces lashed out striking down the knight in his tracks, but the damage had already been done. The Grail King had been struck down.

What the knight had not known was that within this kingdom the land was inseparably tied to the Grail King. As the Grail King fared, so fared the lands.

But now, the Grail King lay struck down in sickness—neither dead, nor truly alive. Because of this, in the kingdom no water flowed, no plants grew, no birds sang. Like the Grail King, the land was neither dead, nor truly alive. In time the kingdom became known as the Waste. Meanwhile, the Grail King knew that all could be as it was before if only a knight could be found with such great valor and inner strength as to brave the Waste and speak the healing words of Truth.

Time came and time went. Years past as time and again brave knights dared the hazards of the Waste. The sheer desolation and loneliness of the land drove many insane before they ever found the castle. Others who were lacking in strength were devoured by the wild beasts that roamed the land. Of the few brave knights that did make it to the castle and entered the chamber of the Grail King, none were pure enough of heart to overcome their awe at the majesty before them. They left—dumbfounded—never to speak again.

Finally a knight came forth with the courage to face the dangers of the Waste. As desolate and lonely as the Waste was, it drove him not mad because he saw beyond the desolation and perceived the plan of the Universe within—and he could find himself to be a part thereof. The wild beasts failed to overcome him, for he knew his strengths and used them well.

At long last he stood in the Chamber of the Grail King. Before him lay the Grail King and on the table the Grail itself. This knight was not overcome by awe because his journey through the Waste had given him valuable lessons bringing forth inner peace and understanding. Standing there, he looked down at the Grail King and asked both of the Grail King—and of himself, "What is the Grail—and whom does it serve?"

Now failure to ask this question would have doomed his valiant quest to failure and the mystery and the kingdom would have gone on as before with no one being served and the kingdom lying in waste. But the question being truthfully spoken aloud invoked to his consciousness the full meanings of all that he had undergone. The spell was broken! Outside it began to rain bringing new life to the land. Within the castle the Grail King rose and took on once more the blushing radiant hue of healthy youth.

So listen, you who would aspire to leadership within the Craft of the Wise. This IS the question which you must truthfully ask of yourself before you step forward and share of the Grail, the Cauldron of Cerridwen. Only you and the Gods will know the answer. "What is the Grail—and whom does it serve?"

In this narration, the High Priest, through the story he relates, gets those who have come to him who believe they are ready for initiation to the Second Degree level of the Craft of the Wise, to search within themselves to find out if they are indeed ready. Working for the attainment of the Second Degree level *is* a quest. The goal is clear, though the path is at times elusive. The classes are at times difficult to comprehend and at other times easy to comprehend, yet, boring to wade through and requiring great stamina.

Just what is this Second Degree level that it would be so difficult, so demanding to achieve?

The Second Degree level of Initiation of the Craft of the Wise is the level at which an individual demonstrates *all* of the qualifications necessary to become a part of the Priesthood. Unfortunately, today within the overall expanse of paganism, the titles of Priest and Priestess have been taken on by many with little training and no desire to serve, but who merely wish to impress others with a title. You can find high school students who have read a few books and have worked what they took from a book verbatim as a Full Moon ritual, who now consider themselves Wiccan Priests or Priestesses! Wow!

There is also a large problem with semantics among the various Wiccan groups. The term Priest or Priestess in proper usage applies only to the male and female leaders of covens who have undergone the necessary training and, in rare cases, to those individuals who have attained the level of the Priesthood but have yet to "hive off" and form their own covens. Yet, there are groups out there who bandy the titles about calling everyone who dedicates a Priest or Priestess to the God and Goddess once they have stood in for either the Priest or the Priestess at a New Moon ritual. This usage would be akin to calling any Catholic who had ever served at a mass a Priest.

The role of Priest or Priestess within the Wiccan religion is a great deal more than just officiating at New Moon and Full Moon rituals. The role is every bit as demanding as that of a Catholic Priest or a Lutheran Minister.

The following are some of the main areas that an individual needs to have the knowledge and ability to handle effectively if they aspire to the Second Degree level.

Priest or Priestess in Ritual

The female initiate must be able to be one with the Goddess in the Circle, and a male one with the God, when the initiate is officiating at a coven celebration. Being one with the God or Goddess is an opening of the inner self that cannot really be described with words. It is a *feeling*. The individual is so opened to the Godhead that he or she can channel the power of the God or Goddess into the Circle and give that power such form that it can be seen, heard and felt by all the others in the Circle. Initiates must have the necessary training to not only open themselves to the Godhead—this is something that almost anyone can do to some degree—but to handle the energy that is channeled down. The power of the Godhead is not something to be played with by those who are incapable of handling its force. Additionally, training—and certainly just being in a ritual circle and opening yourself to the energy being raised is training—should have brought them to a level where they can not only assist in the raising of power within the ritual circle, but also direct and control that power once it has been raised. Again, almost anyone can build energy, but to effectively direct and control that energy so that you—not the energy—is master is not something that just happens. It requires training.

Teacher

Members of a coven look to their Priest and Priestess for education. Both by example in Circle and through formal classes, the Priest and the Priestess must be capable of teaching their coven that which it needs to grow and prosper. The role of teacher is not an easy one to fill. The teacher needs to be well versed in the many areas that need to be covered. Thus, it is helpful that there are two teachers in a coven—a Priest and a Priestess. Each can assist the other to prepare and teach the various classes, with each one teaching the classes in the areas that they are most skilled. The Priest or the Priestess does not have to know everything—only half of everything.

This brings up another point. No one does know everything. More to the point, it is all right for the Priest and the Priestess to admit within a class that they do not know the answer to a question asked by a student. To put the student off with comments like "you will be opened to that later" or "when you are ready the answer will be made clear" does not advance either the student or the teacher. Those who are of the Second Degree level are aware of the value of truth to their students, but even more important, the value of truth to themselves. All unanswered questions can initiate a quest for new knowledge and knowledge is growth.

Counselor

An often overlooked duty of the Priest and the Priestess is counseling. As the religious leaders of a small congregation, a coven, the Priest and Priestess are the people that the rest of the coven should be able to go to for guidance when they have personal problems that they wish to discuss. Therefore, both the Priest and the Priestess should have some outside training in human psychology and should develop the ability to be very objective when counseling people who may be close to them.

The Wiccan Priesthood should always be open to the members of their coven for counseling and guidance. However, the Priesthood should not feel that they have the right to meddle in the lives of coveners. Unless a covener requests counseling, or the personal problem of a covener is affecting the coven's circles, the Priest and the Priestess have no right to interfere with the personal life of any of their coven members. If a personal problem of a covener is seriously creating problems for the coven in Circle, then it is not only the right, but the duty of the Priest or Priestess to intervene and counsel that coven member.

The Priest and the Priestess should also remember that if they are not sure how to handle a particular situation that, with the covener's consent, they have the option of going for advice to the elders who initiated them.

Leader

It may seem redundant after discussing the role of officiate and teacher to bring in leader as a separate role, yet, while leadership is similar and, in part, necessary to officiating and teaching, it *is* distinct from them as well. A person may be a great teacher—able to instill great volumes of knowledge in the classroom—but outside of the classroom be totally ineffective as a leader. In the same vein, an individual in the Circle may be filled by the Goddess and be able to raise and direct fantastic energies, but once outside the Circle, be somewhat lost as to directing anything.

Leadership ability is not something that can be easily taught. Rather, it is a trait that a person with encouragement grows into in time. One of the reasons that it usually takes several years of training to attain the Second Degree level is to allow individuals time to realize their leadership potential. As the Priest or Priestess of a coven, the individual should be ever conscious that all of the coven will look to him or her for an example to follow. To some new dedicants the Priest and the Priestess will seem as Gods. The dedicants may dote on their every word. In these instances it is all too easy for a Priest or Priestess to lose perspective and see his or her leadership ability lost in ego. Be careful!

The leadership of a coven carries with it a responsibility for balance. Neither the Priest nor the Priestess can be overbearing, rather, they need to balance each other out. Those who have achieved the Second Degree level seek to work with—not over—their consort. Whether in Circle, in class, or with the coven at a festival, the Priest and the Priestess should work to complement one another. For the group the Priest and Priestess are two halves of the same whole entity. Together they represent the Great Unmanifest.

These, then, are the main areas of knowledge and ability that the individual needs to develop to achieve the level of Second Degree. For those who do achieve the Second Degree level, who have the knowledge and the experience to be successful in all of these areas, there is still one more thing to do to be initiated into the Priesthood. They need to dedicate their lives to the service of the God, the Goddess, and the coven. Remember, the duties of the Priest or Priestess in the Wiccan religion are no different than, for example, those of the Catholic Priest or the Lutheran Minister. Becoming a Priest or a Priestess in the Wiccan religion means opening yourself to a life of placing the needs of the religion and the coven before your own.

Realizing that there are those who will achieve the level of Second Degree in knowledge and ability but because of personal commitments will be unable to accept the responsibilities of the Priesthood, the First Temple of the Craft of W.I.C.A. has two slightly different initiation ceremonies for the Second Degree level.

One initiation ceremony is used for those individuals who have reached the level of Second Degree and are willing to make the commitment to dedicate their lives to the service of the God and Goddess by being initiated into the priesthood. The ceremony brings to consciousness the seriousness of the commitment that the initiate is about to take. The ceremony also forms a formal bond between the new initiate to the priesthood and the lineage of Priests and Priestesses participating in the initiation ceremony.

The second type of initiation ceremony is used for those individuals who have attained the level of Second Degree but because of personal commitments feel that they would not be able to live up to the full responsibilities of the priesthood. Declining the role of Priest or Priestess should not be held against them. Many of those who have declined initiation into the priesthood still work hard in the Wiccan religion by teaching within the coven and assisting the Priest and Priestess.

In this second type of initiation ceremony the emphasis is on the level of awareness that the individual has reached. It concentrates on the harmony the individual has worked for to achieve that awareness and opens the person for continued growth in the future. Even though they have not been brought into the priesthood, those individuals who have gone through this second form of initiation are Second Degree Initiates!

For those readers who are expecting to find a complete Second Degree Initiation ritual at this point, I am sorry to disappoint you—but I must!

As I mentioned earlier in this chapter, the pagan community abounds with those who claim the title of Priest or Priestess with little or no knowledge or training to verify their claim. If I were to make the complete Second Degree Initiation ritual open and public, I would only be compounding the problem. There would be those who would pick up the book, flip to the last chapter, talk themselves through the ritual, and claim to be part of the priesthood—able to quote from the ritual to "verify" their claim.

For those who are practicing solitary who desire to enter the priesthood with the hope of leading a coven, I suggest you make contact with a coven near you and see about taking the classes necessary to achieve entrance into the priesthood. If there are no groups within a practical travel distance, there is, of course, the possibility of conversing by mail. For those readers in the Midwest who are too distant from a coven for classes or who have no contacts to try, please write to me in care of the First Temple of the Craft of W.I.C.A. Because of its involvement with the Midwest Pagan Council, the First Temple of the Craft of W.I.C.A. may be able to help you make a contact in your area.

Blessed Be!

Epilogue

It may seem to some readers that by the time an individual reaches the level of Second Degree they have achieved all that there is to achieve and should be able to walk on water. Nothing could be further from the truth.

The chapters on both the First Degree level and the Second Degree level cover some of the wide range of knowledge and ability that a person should achieve in order to attain the level of awareness indicated by the degree. There will be required areas that a person may excel in and other areas where he or she just gets by. Once people are initiated into a degree level, they must fine tune those areas that they excel in and learn and work more on those areas where they are just getting by. In the same vein, life is not a constant—everyone has ups and downs. Once a person achieves a particular level of awareness, this does not mean that they can let it go and stop working on it. Like a bodybuilder who must continue exercising to maintain muscle fitness, once the spiritual faculties are developed, if they are then left unused, they will atrophy. To maintain awareness, the faculties must be used and worked on regularly.

All of life is a learning experience that instills growth in one way or another. No matter what degree level a person may have reached or how much wisdom they may have accumulated, so long as there is life, there is always more to learn. After twenty-five years of reading, teaching, and working within the Craft, there are classes that I give in which a question or a statement by a student opens for me a whole new area of consciousness and gives to me a whole new learning quest. Many years ago I started referring to classes as a "mutual learning exchange." At times it is hard to determine just who is learning more in a particular class—the student or the teacher!

So, for those who feel that by reaching the level of Second Degree they "have it made" and can now rest on their laurels, I leave you with the words (that I now have on a sign leading down to the Temple area) given to me by Cathy, a Temple member,

NO REST FOR THE WICCA'D!

Glossary

Because some readers may be new to Wicca and unfamiliar with some of the terms used in this book, we have included a glossary to assist in the understanding of those terms. It is important to remember that the definitions given are those used by the First Temple of the Craft of W.I.C.A. and that other groups may vary in defining the same terms.

Athame: The traditional black-handled knife used in the Wiccan religion for ritual work in the Circle. As it is designated for ritual use only, the edges of the athame should not be sharpened. Before its first ritual use, the athame should be purified and consecrated. The athame is an extension of the individual that is used to direct and focus his or her energy. As such, the blade should be made from a conductive material. The materials we suggest in ascending order—from least preferable to most preferable—are steel, brass, copper, silver, or gold. Of recent note are some expensive athames made with blades of quartz crystal. As quartz crystal is a frequency resonator more aligned to reception than to transmission, its use in this instance is questionable.

Aura: The electromagnetic field that surrounds the physical form of all beings.

Auric Shield: Similar to an invisible fine network webbing, the auric shield is the outer containment surface of the aura.

Censer: Another name for an incense burner, though in most instances this one is like a bowl with or without a rounded top with vent holes. A censer is normally made of brass or fired ceramic. The base of the censer is usually filled with sand,

and a piece of self-lighting charcoal (available from most supply shops or bookstores that carry Wiccan supplies). The charcoal is topped with the incense resin of your choice.

Channeling: The ability of a person to be the conductor for energy or entities to be brought into the Circle. Within the Circle there are times that the Priest will act as a channel for the God-force and the Priestess as a channel for the Goddess-force.

Coven: A formal Wiccan group, led by a Priestess and a Priest, that celebrates the Festivals and the Moons. Members of a coven all go through the same orientation, so that in Circle they are balanced and can work together.

Elements: Earth, Water, Fire, Air—plus Spirit—are considered the elements that make up all that is life. In magick, the elements represent the different categories and levels of manifestation. Earth represents material form—the "here and now." Water is the emotional flow in life. Fire is the very activity of life itself. Air is the thought and inspiration behind all of manifested existence. Spirit is the guiding force that binds the other four elements to create positive existence.

Handfasting: This is the term used for marriage in the Wiccan religion. The term derives from an old European custom of binding the couple's hands together to symbolize their union. The handfasting can be done to signify a union between two people for a year and a day—after which time the vows may be renewed—or a permanent union for "so long as life and love shall last."

Hexagram: The hexagram is the six-pointed star. It is also known as the Star of David and the Greater Seal of Solomon. Comprised of two interlocked triangles, it portrays the "As Above, So Below" principle of magick. When reference in this book is made to "doing an invoking Hexagram," the celebrant stands facing the direction indicated, and starting with both hands together before the body, brings them apart and down to form the two sides of the upper triangle. The hands are then brought together to form the bottom of the upper triangle. Hands still together, the celebrant then brings their hands to a point just above the bottom side of the upper triangle. The hands are spread apart in a straight line to form the bottom of the lower triangle. From here, the hands are brought down and together to form the remaining two sides of the lower triangle. A dismissing hexagram is done by reversing the procedure starting with the hands together at the bottom (point) of the lower triangle.

Invocation: The calling forth or calling in of an entity or presence is known as an invocation. It is a formal invitation for the entity's presence.

Magick: The art of causing coincidence to occur at will with or without formal physical ritual. To distinguish magick from magic (sleight of hand illusion) a *k* is added to the end of the word.

Pentacle: A talisman, usually round, inscribed with a five-pointed star or a five-pointed star inside of a circle. In the Wiccan religion it can be used to signify the Earth element.

Pentagram: The five-pointed star used in magick and Wicca for invoking and dismissing the elements. It is also known as the Lesser Seal of Solomon. With the single point upward it is a symbolic representation of humankind. The invoking pentagrams for the elements are done as follows:

> *Air*: Stand in the east with your athame and draw the pentagram before you, starting with the point upper right, going in order to the point upper left, lower right, top center, lower left, and back to upper right.

> *Fire*: Stand in the south with your athame and draw the pentagram before you, starting with the top center point, going in order to the point lower right, upper left, upper right, lower left, and back to the top center point.

Water: Stand in the west with your athame and draw the pentagram before you, starting with the point upper left, going in order to the point upper right, lower left, top center, lower right, and back to upper left.

Earth: Stand in the north with your athame and draw the pentagram before you, starting with the top center point, going in order to the point lower left, upper right, upper left, lower right, and back to the top center point.

Active Spirit: Stand before the altar with your athame and draw the pentagram before you, starting with the lower right, going in order to the point upper left, upper right, lower left, top center, and back to the lower right.

Passive Spirit: Stand before the altar with your athame and draw the pentagram before you, starting with the lower left, going in order to the point upper right, upper left, lower right, top center, and back to the lower left.

The dismissing pentagrams for the elements are done as follows:

Air: Stand in the east with your athame and draw the pentagram before you, starting with the point upper left, going in order to the point upper right, lower left, top center, lower right, and back to the upper left point.

Fire: Stand in the south with your athame and draw the pentagram before you, starting with the point lower right, going in order to the point top center, lower left, upper right, upper left, and back down to the lower right point.

Water: Stand in the west with your athame and draw the pentagram before you, starting with the point upper right, going in order to the point upper left, lower right, top center, lower left, and back to upper right.

Earth: Stand in the north with your athame and draw the pentagram before you, starting with the point lower left, going in order to the point top center, lower right, upper left, upper right, and back down to the lower left point.

Active Spirit: Stand before the altar with your athame and draw the pentagram before you, starting with the point upper left, going in order to the point lower right, top center, lower left, upper right, and back across to the upper left point.

Passive Spirit: Stand before the altar with your athame and draw the pentagram before you, starting with the point upper right, going in order to the point lower left, top center, lower right, upper left, and back across to the upper right point.

Qabala: An ancient mystical system of defining, identifying, and working with the various aspects of the godhead. While predominantly passed down through Hebrew teachings and rabbinical texts, its actual origin is unknown and predates by centuries any of the Hebrew works it may be found in. It is the basis for most Western esoteric schools of magick.

Watcher: This is another name for the elemental guardians invoked to protect the Circle. Also known as the "Old Ones."

Wicca: The Craft of the Wise is known as Wicca. Another name for Wicca is Witchcraft.

Wiccaning: A ritual in the Wiccan religion wherein the God and the Goddess are called forth to give their protection and spiritual aid to a young child until such time as that child is able to knowingly choose his or her own spiritual path. It is similar to a christening.

Witch: One skilled in the lore of Witchcraft, i.e., Wicca. Usually the Priestess and Priest of a Coven are Witches.

Stanley J. A. Modrzyk opened Sanctus Spiritus, an Occult-Astrological supply shop, in 1970. Through the shop he provided contacts for anyone interested in the Magickal Arts. Through these contacts the First Temple of the Craft of W.I.C.A. was born and incorporated as a church under Illinois law in 1972.

In 1976, Modrzyk helped create the Midwest Pagan Council. He has been an officer of the Council and is a member of its Board of Directors. He is an active member who writes a column for the quarterly newsletter, *Midwest Pagan Correspondence*, and helps run the Pan Pagan Festival each summer. Dedicated to educating the public about modern Witchcraft, Modrzyk frequently speaks at universities and public seminars, and has been featured in newspapers and national magazines, and on television and radio talk shows. His previous work, *Turning of the Wheel*, also available from Samuel Weiser, has been lauded by the Pagan community as a book long overdue. Mr. Modrzyk is currently producing a series of "How to" videotapes on various esoteric topics.

If there were questions brought to consciousness by this book, please feel free to address them to the author at the following address:

P. O. Box 59
Western Springs, IL 60558-0059.

Please allow ample time for a response.

Blessed Be!